THE FURNACE OF AFFLICTION

"If you have ever questioned God's love for you when you are suffering, this story will encourage and challenge you. Horace shares the struggles he has faced and how God uses and redeems our pain."

—**SHEILA WALSH**, co-host of Life Today and author of *Praying Women*

"Horace Williams Jr. takes us on a journey through the scriptures as well as his own experiences to contemplate the causes and purposes of pain and sorrow. The book is filled with the constant encouragement to consider God's sovereign work for His glory and for our good, even in our most difficult times of suffering. It culminates with a hopeful and comforting chapter on the destiny of all Christians: a glorious, joyful gathering with Christ, where sin and pain are forever banished."

—**DANIEL SWEET**, senior pastor, Matthew Road Baptist Church

"*The Furnace of Affliction* gives us an in-depth view of how God uses and even orchestrates times of pain and sorrow to refine us into the image of Christ. Horace Williams Jr. shares honest insight into his own life and relies heavily on scripture, making the book a powerful must-read for anyone who has ever felt abandoned by God or struggled to reconcile His love with a world full of suffering."

—**PHIL MCGLOTHLIN**, associate pastor, Matthew Road Baptist Church

THE
FURNACE
OF AFFLICTION

How God Uses
Our Pain and Suffering
for His Purpose

HORACE WILLIAMS JR.

Published by Black Lillie Press

Editing: Megan Langston, www.meganlangstoncopy.com
Proofreading: Lisa Thompson, www.writebylisa.com
Publishing and Design Services: Melinda Martin, MartinPublishingServices.com
Front Cover Design: Jonathan Lewis, jonlincreative.com

ISBN: 978-0-9997599-2-9 (paperback), 978-0-9997599-3-6 (epub), 978-0-9997599-4-3 (mobi)

To those who've been hurt, are living in pain, or are suffering in silence: May this book give you comfort and encourage you. I pray that the heavenly Father showers you with His peace and caresses your heart with His love as you realize God's purpose for your life.

CONTENTS

GOD USES PAIN AND SUFFERING TO:

Introduction

Pain. It is not a word we like to hear or something we enjoy experiencing. In my research over the past few years, I have discovered that many people are unwilling to admit they've faced pain. They may be too hurt or afraid to express the pain they are feeling. They might even be fearful of being mocked, ridiculed, or seen as weak.

However, feeling pain is a fact of life. At some point, we will have to confront it. During the decades God has blessed me with life on this earth, I have experienced pain and suffering in varying degrees.

I vividly remember when a playmate unintentionally split open my forehead in the sandbox when I was four years old. I staggered to the back door of my house, screaming. Blood was streaming down my face. To this day, I have a small scar to remind me of that traumatic event.

I also remember the pain and humiliation of not being able to walk with my classmates for my high school graduation. The discipline involved my attendance at summer school that year. I received my diploma in the mail three months after the ceremony, a few days after my sixteenth birthday.

As a young adult, I remember the agony of being in love and losing that love—I was curled up in a fetal position, crying like a newborn baby because the person I was engaged to be married to had walked away.

In my mid-twenties, I endured heart-wrenching sorrow at my grandmother's funeral while reciting a poem I'd written about her. She helped raise me, and I spent time caring for her in her later years after her stroke. I became so overwhelmed and was hurting so deeply that I had to fight through my sobbing to finish the poem.

When it comes to my career, even though I've been successful in my almost twenty years in sales and marketing, I carry with me the unexpected and painful experience of being let go from a job. Twice.

We all experience pain in some form or fashion, whether it be chronic physical or emotional pain. We also experience spiritual pain through spiritual warfare as we seek to live for Christ.

I battle with debilitating physical pain every day. Because it has become so familiar to me, I am comfortable talking about it.

The pain I feel is a result of a massive hemorrhagic stroke that I suffered in the summer of 2010—July 1 is a day I will never forget.

While talking to a colleague at the office that day, I dropped the gum bottle I was holding. He called me clumsy and asked me what was wrong. I told him I didn't feel well and asked him to take me home. I didn't realize that the left side of my mouth had begun to droop. Another friend came into my office. I had gotten off the phone with her a few moments earlier, and she was concerned because I sounded funny. I thought she was teasing me, but she dialed 9-1-1 right away when she realized something was terribly wrong; she probably helped saved my life.

In what seemed like an instant, I was on my way to the hospital. When I arrived, I struggled franticly with the nurses as they tried to prepare me for a CT scan. I was desperate to communicate that I was claustrophobic as they attempted to put me into the machine. Then I felt something hit my arm—possibly an injection of some kind—and I was out like a light.

I awakened days later in a dimly lit hospital room with my right leg tethered to the bed to prevent blood clotting. I couldn't sit up, and I screamed for help. A nurse quickly came in, saw I was awake, and went to get the doctor.

The doctor informed me about the stroke and said that my left side had been paralyzed when a blood vessel burst on the right side of my brain.

My vision was blurry, and I was in a fog for several weeks afterward. I couldn't walk and was introduced to a wheelchair.

To this day, the nerves on the left side of my body radiate through me like electricity. I can't use my left hand to type or hold anything fragile, and the joints on my left side are as stiff as boards from head to toe. Over nine years after the stroke, I still sleep with my left leg elevated to help with blood flow and to minimize the agonizing nerve pain. I never thought I would miss being able to drive a stick shift automobile, wiggle my toes, or bend my foot down into a shoe.

Shortly after my stroke, my mother expressed concern to the doctor at a follow-up visit about the hydrocodone that was part of my prescription regimen.

She was afraid I could become addicted to such a potent opioid. The doctor explained to her that the nerve pains some stroke victims experience are like what you would feel sticking your foot in a pot of boiling water. Finally, someone could articulate the pain I was experiencing—the pain is not like a charley horse or the pain you feel when you hit your funny bone. It is excruciating, searing, relentless pain.

My mother looked at me, and I winked and nodded in agreement with the doctor. The sadness in her eyes was evident as she began to understand the severity of the pain I was trying to manage.

As time went by and I tried to return to a normal life, I had to retake my driving test—I did not want to endanger myself or anyone else. I passed the exam, praise God, and I have been off hydrocodone ever since that test.

I'm learning to live with the pain, and only because of God's strength am I able to make it through each day.

So how does God use pain? Would He get our attention without it? I know that when everything was rainbows and unicorns for me, I made no time for God. My relationship with Him was distant at best.

Of course, since I was raised in a Christian home and dragged to church every Sunday as a child, I knew plenty about God. I even asked Jesus Christ to come into my heart and save me at the age of five.

However, for the thirty-eight years of my life that followed, I tried to do everything on my own. I was self-motivated, selfish, driven to succeed, and headed away from God. Self-motivation and drive are fantastic, but when we are focused on ourselves and not on living for God, adversity will block our paths to real success.

It's beyond disappointing that none of the painful moments I'd endured before the stroke were enough to turn my attention toward God. Only after the stroke when my physical pain and suffering became constant did I decide to recommit to God.

I would lay awake in the hospital at night, not believing what had happened. The pain and humiliation of not being able to care for myself was devastating. I struggled to recite Psalm 23, hindered by my injured brain. I had not prayed with any sincerity in several years, but I asked God for help and healing. I struggled internally, asking why this happened, but in reality, I knew the answer—I had been living a selfish life infused with worldly desires.

In that painful and isolated moment, God spoke to me. He revealed that His desire was not for me to live for myself or to accumulate wealth and things of no heavenly value but to live a life that glorifies Him—to share my testimony of faith with all who will listen (and even those who won't). He saved me from eternal damnation, not so that I'd "stay out of hell," but so that I'd help people know Him and inspire them to live for Christ.

This story of redemption is why I have written this book—not to join you in a pit of misery. But I hope to lift your spirits, encourage your heart, and challenge you to look deep within yourself, despite the painful trials you encounter.

My intent is not to minimize or trivialize your pain; I intend to give you hope amid your suffering. God has a plan and a purpose for your life (Jeremiah 29:11, author's paraphrase). It may be hard to see through the tears that moisten your face at times, but I speak from experience—God wants what is best for you.

The transformation may involve spending time in the furnace of affliction. God will keep you there as long as it takes to accomplish His will and plan for you.

British author C. S. Lewis states in *The Problem of Pain*, "We can ignore even pleasure. But pain insists upon being attended to. God whispers to us in our pleasures, speaks to us in our conscience, but shouts in our pains: it is His megaphone to rouse a deaf world."[1]

Does God seem to be shouting at you through pain and suffering? Have you been listening, or have you been hard of hearing in your walk with Him?

God is just and righteous, and God is holy. Thankfully, He is compassionate as well. His desire is not to do you harm but to conform you to His image.

One of my favorite passages of Scripture, which I committed to memory during the early stages of my spiritual transformation, is this: "And we know that God causes all things to work together for good to those who love God, to those who are called according to His purpose" (Romans 8:28).

However, the verses that follow are often forgotten or ignored. Read these and commit them to memory. "For those whom He foreknew, He also predestined to become conformed to the image of His Son, so that He would be the firstborn among many brethren; and these whom He predestined, He also called; and these whom He called, He also justified; and these whom He justified, He also glorified. What then shall we say to these things? If God is for us, who is against us?" (Romans 8:29–31).

From the moment we accepted Jesus Christ as our Lord and Savior, we were justified by God through the blood of Jesus Christ and that alone. However, that does not exempt us from experiencing time in the furnace of affliction.

---

1 C. S. Lewis, *The Problem of Pain* (Québec: Samizdat University Press, 1940), 57–58.

God sometimes uses pain to help us develop an intimate relationship with Him. He also uses pain and suffering—our time in the furnace of affliction—to do the following:

- divulge sin in our lives
- develop our faith
- demolish our pride
- determine our paths
- demonstrate His grace
- display His love
- deepen our commitment to Him
- deliver hope, comfort, and joy

We will discuss each of these in this book.

It is my prayer that you will take this time to honestly evaluate your times of anguish and be filled with hope as you begin to understand God's intent for your life.

Join me, and we'll walk through this journey of pain and suffering together.

THE ORIGIN OF SUFFERING

Suffering. Before I explain how God uses our pain for His purpose, I want to explore the word "suffering." What does it mean to you?

You might have experienced physical pain or maybe even the rarely discussed emotional distress. What about spiritual pain? This is the internal conflict between you and God as your transforming heart battles to live for Christ. The struggle is real for us while living in the corruptness of a human body.

Our sinful nature is a result of what took place in the garden of Eden. From the moment Adam and Eve disobeyed God and ate from the tree of the Knowledge of Good and Evil, they became separated from God. "They heard the sound of the Lord God walking in the garden in the cool of the day, and the man and his wife hid themselves from the presence of the Lord God among the trees of the garden" (Genesis 3:8).

While taking turns in the blame game, Adam blamed the woman and God, and Eve blamed the serpent (Satan). God put an end to the blaming and cursed everyone involved. This was the origin of suffering.

> To the woman He said, "I will greatly multiply your pain in childbirth, in pain you will bring forth children; yet your desire will be for your husband, and he will rule over you. Then to Adam He said, "Because you have listened to the voice of your wife, and have eaten from the tree about which I commanded you, saying, 'You shall not eat from it'; cursed is the ground because of you; in toil you will eat of it all the days of your life. 'Both thorns and thistles it shall grow for you; and you will eat the plants of the field; by the sweat of your face you will eat bread, till you return to the ground because from it you were taken; for you are dust, and to dust you shall return'" (Genesis 3:16–19).

Despite what took place in the garden, God still desires to have an intimate relationship with us. That is why He sent His Son, Jesus, to die on the cross for our sins. His perfect sacrifice gives us the opportunity for fellowship with Him.

Know that pain is not meant to destroy us but to develop us. God wants to use us for His glory. However, to be suitable vessels for Him, we must spend time being transformed in the furnace of affliction. "Not only that, but we rejoice in our sufferings, knowing that suffering produces endurance, and endurance produces character, and character produces hope, and hope does not put us to shame, because God's love has been poured into our hearts through the Holy Spirit who has been given to us" (Romans 5:3–5 ESV).

In that painful and
isolated moment,
God spoke to me.

MY PRAYER

Dear heavenly Father, I am humbled to share some of my moments in the furnace of affliction with those who love You. Thank You for Your desire to continue working on us, Your children, molding, shaping, and preparing us for Your glory. I pray that You will give those of us who are hurting or who have experienced suffering, Your indescribable peace, a peace beyond all understanding. Guard our hearts, Lord. Give us the wisdom we need, which You offer up generously to everyone who asks. Encourage us every step of the way as we seek to live for You. May our lives bring glory to You and draw others to Christ. In Jesus' name, I pray. Amen.

1

GOD USES OUR PAIN AND SUFFERING TO

DIVULGE SIN IN OUR LIVES

As far back as biblical times, people often assumed that suffering from some physical infirmity or difficulty was a direct result of sin in your life. If you have never accepted Jesus Christ as your personal Lord and Savior, God might indeed use pain to help you recognize your need for Him.

You may attempt to camouflage the sins in your life by comparing yourself to the criminals and evildoers that litter our newscasts daily. However, as God states in His Word, that is not the standard to compare yourself to. "For all have sinned and fall short of the glory of God" (Romans 3:23).

God's desire is for each of us to come to Him willingly and seek forgiveness for our sins. Only then can we enter into a personal relationship with Jesus Christ. Because of Adam's sin in the garden of Eden, we are infected with a sin nature. In fact, we were born with it.

Now before you object, consider this: Does a child have to be taught how to be selfish or to tell a lie?

Usually, one of the first words a child speaks after mumbling out some version of mommy or daddy is "mine!" If you still refuse to admit you're a sinner, that may be the exact reason God has you in the furnace of affliction. He wants your attention. He desires to welcome you into His family. However, sometimes it takes painful situations to grab your attention and remind you that you need the Savior, Jesus Christ.

Being a Christian is more than living a "pretty good" life while being kind to others or going to church regularly. God wants us to have a heart change—a willingness to live for and obey Him.

If you are reading this book and have not admitted to God that you are a sinner and asked Him to forgive you of your sins and come into your heart, you are in for a lot worse than time in the furnace of affliction.

UNQUENCHABLE FIRE

If you continue to refuse your need for the Savior, you are destined to spend eternity in hell. That is not my opinion; it comes directly from the Bible. Hell is not fiction or a fairy tale. Hell is a real place where all who have refused Christ as their Savior will spend eternity.

"Do not fear those who kill the body and are unable to kill the soul, but rather fear Him who is able to destroy both the body and soul in hell" (Matthew 10:28).

"His winnowing fork is in His hand and He will thoroughly clear His threshing floor; and He will gather His wheat into the barn, but He will burn up the chaff with unquenchable fire" (Matthew 3:12).

God is holy, and He cannot tolerate sin. That is why He sent His Son, Jesus Christ, to walk the earth in human form and allowed Him to die on the cross and rise from the grave three days later.

It took the sacrifice of the perfect Savior to cover the sins of humankind. However, you must accept this gift of salvation, not only to be rescued from eternal damnation but to live in concert with Him.

I pray that if you don't know Jesus Christ as your Savior, that you will confess your sins and ask Him to be Lord of your life. Salvation is not a guarantee that your life will always be comfortable. It does mean that you have almighty God living within you through the Holy Spirit.

Christians Are Sinners Too

At the age of five, I knelt next to my bed with my mother beside me and asked Jesus to come into my heart. More than anything else, I knew I was deathly afraid of going to hell. However, throughout middle school, junior high, and high school, I had no heart transformation.

I was dragged to Sunday school and church every time the doors were open, but I had no desire to develop my relationship with God. I was not living a Christ-like life, so a lot of my pain and suffering leading up to my stroke was self-inflicted.

As painful as those trying seasons in my life were, I feel I have learned and grown from the experiences. I no longer practice those habitual sins, taking advantage of God's undeserved grace. "No one who is born of God practices sin, because His seed abides in him; and he cannot sin, because he is born of God" (1 John 3:9).

As born-again Christians, we should have a heart change resulting in a shift in our behaviors as we seek to live for Christ.

Transformation takes place in our hearts with the help of the Holy Spirit as we immerse ourselves in God's Word and seek to understand His commandments. When we are too busy or unwilling to do so, God will get our attention.

Here are some of my favorite verses from Psalm 119. They spoke to me loudly after my stroke as I dove into the Bible to understand and know God's purpose for my life.

"Before I was afflicted I went astray, but now I keep Your word. You are good and do good; teach me Your statutes . . . . With all my heart I will observe Your precepts. It is good for me that I was afflicted, that I may learn Your statutes . . . . Your hands made me and fashioned me. Give me understanding, that I may learn Your commandments . . . . I know, O Lord, that Your judgments are righteous, and in faithfulness You have afflicted me" (Psalm 119:67–69, 71, 73, 75).

When I read these passages for the first time, everything began to come into focus. I had forgotten or ignored all God's precepts that I had heard and memorized as a child. (I especially ignored them in my teenage and adult years—ask any of my family members. Or maybe you shouldn't.)

I did everything I could to avoid the conviction of the Holy Spirit. This included not reading my Bible regularly. I also resisted going to church as often as possible, and in doing so, I missed fellowship with other Christians and the teaching of God's Word.

I kept busy with my work—I was convinced that I was doing the right thing in providing for myself. Meanwhile, I forgot that it was God who had blessed me with the talents and abilities to thrive in my profession. I lived a self-indulgent, believe-only-in-myself lifestyle until it all came crashing down on me in the form of a life-altering stroke.

The furnace of affliction is a constant tool God uses while we are here on earth. We will experience pain and suffering until He takes us to heaven to live with Him. How long we spend in the furnace has a lot to do with how we respond to God's ongoing attempts to make us more like Him.

God does not want a bunch of robots walking around saying, "Yes, Master; what can I do, Master?" God has given us a choice—a choice to live a life that pleases and glorifies Him.

God wants to purify us from sin. This is His first step in fulfilling His purpose in our pain.

Our earthly bodies are dying a little bit each day. However, the Holy Spirit lives within us, convicting us of sin and empowering us to live for Christ.

So let me ask you this: can you give up those habitual sins willingly, or do you prefer some prodding from God? I highly recommend you surrender those sins. Look at the decision that King David made after realizing God knew of his sin.

"When I kept silent about my sin, my body wasted away through my groaning all day long. For day and night Your hand was heavy upon me; My vitality was drained away as with the fever heat of summer. I acknowledged my sin to You, and my iniquity I did not hide. I said, 'I will confess my transgressions to the Lord;' and You forgave the guilt of my sin (Psalm 32:3–5).

Now, you may be wondering, "Why all this talk about sin?" My dear brother or sister in Christ, God wants to use us for His glory, and He cannot use us if we continue to live in sin. Period.

I'm speaking from experience. Don't fall into the trap of believing that you are without sin.

DESTRUCTIVE SINS THAT INTERFERE WITH OUR RELATIONSHIP WITH GOD

PRIDE

I must continually guard against this sneaky sin. I have been self-assured most of my life. Excelling in athletics during high school gave me extreme confidence as a teenager. As an adult, monetary success and recognition in the corporate world went straight to my head.

I was extremely proud of my accomplishments, but something was missing.

I rarely, if ever, gave God the glory. When we attempt to do things using our own strength without consulting and including God, that is pride. When we pat ourselves on the back without thanking Him, that, too, is pride.

A fine line exists between the self-indulgent pride that comes with an accomplishment and the pride we feel when God blesses us with the ability and talents to achieve said accomplishment.

You will read more about pride as we move on. In the meantime, think about how easy it is to be prideful and not live with a heart of gratitude toward God.

COMPLAINING

This is another one of those sneaky sins that we can quickly fall into a habit of committing daily. We can complain about something from sunrise to sunset without even realizing we are doing so. We may grumble while getting up in the morning. Then we moan about the traffic on the way to work or school. Then we criticize our workloads.

Think about the Israelites and how they behaved on the way to the promised land. After being rescued from slavery and escaping Pharaoh and the Egyptians, they complained repeatedly along their journey.

"The whole congregation of the sons of Israel grumbled against Moses and Aaron in the wilderness. The sons of Israel said to them, 'Would that we had died by the Lord's hand in the land of Egypt, when we sat by the pots of meat, when we ate bread to the full; for you have brought us out into this wilderness to kill this whole assembly with hunger'" (Exodus 16:2–3).

Grumbling and complaining is blatant disrespect toward God. Because of Him, we woke up this morning. He has blessed us with the ability to read, write, think for ourselves, and earn a living. He allows us to care for our children and loved ones. He has granted us gifts, talents, and abilities that we use every day. We choose to be disrespectful and dismissive of those blessings when we complain.

Beware of the negative self-talk that permeates your mind and makes its way into the world. God hears everything you say and knows your heart. Complaining is a destructive habit that can quickly become part of your DNA if you're not careful; it is not representative of who you are intended to be in Christ.

"Now the people became like those who complain of adversity in the hearing of the Lord, and when the Lord heard it, His anger was kindled, and the fire of the Lord burned among them and consumed some of the outskirts of the camp. The people therefore cried out to Moses, and Moses prayed to the Lord and the fire died out" (Numbers 11:1–2).

"Do all things without grumbling or disputing; so that you will prove yourselves to be blameless and innocent, children of God above reproach in the midst of a crooked and perverse generation, among whom you appear as lights in the world" (Philippians 2:14–15).

SELFISHNESS

Selfishness has been a life-long battle for me. Some of the best times in my life were the years as a toddler before my younger brother was born. I was the center of attention for my grandmother and her best friend across the street as they helped care for me.

They spoiled me rotten and gave me whatever I wanted, which most days was a "hamboogie and chee-chees" or in "adult speak," a hamburger and Cheetos. Yum!

Three years later, when my first sibling was born, I had to learn the dreaded word "share." We shared a bedroom, we shared clothes, and we even shared the bathtub.

Now don't get me wrong, this was nowhere near a Cain-and-Abel situation. I loved and still do love my brother dearly. We grew thick as thieves over time, and I missed him terribly when he joined the US Marine Corps. However, I struggled with living selfishly for many years. It is only by God's grace that my selfish monster doesn't rear its ugly head daily.

A painful realization is that selfishness is probably one of the reasons I have remained single for all these years. We must willingly purpose to live selflessly, putting the needs of others ahead of our desires, which I had long failed to do. "Do nothing from selfishness or empty conceit, but with humility of mind regard one another as more important than yourselves; do not merely look for your own personal interests, but also for the interests of others" (Philippians 2:3–4).

Pride, complaining, and selfishness are three sneaky or presumptuous sins that will directly affect our time spent in the furnace of affliction. The purifying process, though necessary, can be piercingly painful as God seeks to remove sin from our lives.

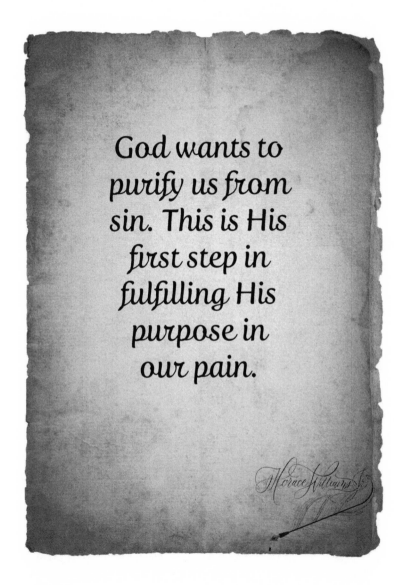

God wants to purify us from sin. This is His first step in fulfilling His purpose in our pain.

REFINING FIRE QUESTIONS

Are you hurting right now (or have you suffered painful situations in the past)? What type of pain are you experiencing: physical, emotional, or spiritual? Answering these questions is the beginning of seeing God's purpose in your circumstances.

_____

_____

_____

Have you accepted Christ as your personal Lord and Savior, asking Him to forgive you of your sins and come live within your heart? If you have not, what is holding you back?

_____

_____

_____

Are you battling any sneaky sins? What sins are you battling that I didn't mention? What is God saying to you about those sins right now?

_____

_____

_____

Search me, O God, and know my heart; try me and know
my anxious thoughts; And see if there be any hurtful way
in me and lead me in the everlasting way.

Psalm 139:23–24

2

GOD USES OUR PAIN AND SUFFERING TO

DEVELOP OUR FAITH

When we accept Christ as our personal Lord and Savior, we experience "saving faith."

We believe that Jesus came to earth as a baby and that He died on a cross thirty-three years later as a sacrifice for our sins. He was raised from the dead and now sits on a throne in heaven at the right hand of God. However, from the moment we made that decision to trust in Him as our Savior, we became an enemy of Satan, whose fate was sealed the moment Christ rose from the dead. Satan is fully aware that an eternity in hell awaits him.

Satan will bombard us with temptations to steer us away from the path that God has planned.

"Be of sober spirit, be on the alert. Your adversary, the devil, prowls around like a roaring lion, seeking someone to devour. But resist him, *firm in your faith*, knowing that the same experiences of suffering are being accomplished by your brethren who are in the world. After you have suffered for a little while, the God of all grace, who called you to His eternal glory in Christ, will Himself perfect, confirm, strengthen, and establish you" (1 Peter 5:8–10, emphasis added).

Wow. These three verses give us a lot to digest. This passage of Scripture is one of the first that I committed to memory after my stroke. It reminds me that I am not the only Christian to experience pain and suffering, and I won't be the last. It also paints a visceral picture of the devil roaming around, looking for the next meal—someone he can rip into shreds!

The beautiful thing about Scripture is that regardless of the stark reality God reveals to us in His Word, He never leaves us without hope. Our suffering will not last forever. God is using our pain to strengthen us for everything He knows we will encounter in the future.

Okay, so we know about saving faith, and as God seeks to strengthen our faith, He develops it through trials. What the devil uses to tempt us, God uses as tests to fortify our faith.

Think back to the Israelites and their journey through the desert. "Then the Lord said to Moses, 'Behold, I will rain bread from heaven for you; and the people shall go out and gather a day's portion every day, that I may test them, whether or not they will walk in My instruction'" (Exodus 16:4).

Just as God equips us to defend ourselves against the enemy, our time spent in the furnace of affliction strengthens our faith. He desires to elevate us from saving faith to an entirely different level that equips us for the journey called life.

Of the many people who come to mind when I think of faith, one of the first is Abram, who became Abraham after God changed his name. He had to go through various stages of faith before God could accomplish everything He intended in Abraham's life.

When we first read of Abram in the Bible, God had instructed him to leave his family and home. Although Abram had no idea where God was leading him, he went willingly with no questions asked. This is an example of solid faith.

"Now the Lord said to Abram, 'Go forth from your country, and from your relatives and from your father's house, to the land which I will show you; and I will make you a great nation, and I will bless you, and make your name great; and so you shall be a blessing . . . . So, Abram went forth as the Lord had spoken to him.'" (Genesis 12:1–2, 4)

The Bible makes no mention of Abram calling friends for their thoughts on what God instructed him to do. He did not check his horoscope in the paper while drinking his morning coffee. He just went. Abraham passed this test with flying colors.

Faith takes time to develop, so prepare yourself to spend time in the furnace throughout your life. God is always at work on your transformation from a sinner headed to hell to a sainted vessel that He can use for His glory.

STRONG FAITH

God promised Abraham and his wife, Sarah, that they would have a son even though they both were advanced in age. He was approaching one hundred years old, and Sarah was not far behind. Abraham believed the Lord, and the Bible states it was counted to him as righteousness (Genesis 15:6).

Strong faith is empowering, and God desires much more for us. He wants to take us higher. Remember our adversary, the devil? He has not forgotten about you and me. Two favorite weapons that Satan uses to attack and destroy us are doubt and discouragement.

Though Abraham believed God, after ten years of waiting for a child, he and Sarah became discouraged. He listened to his wife's suggestion and had sexual relations with his wife's maid, Hagar, in a foolish attempt to have the child God promised. Hagar did become pregnant and gave birth to a son, but that was not the heir that God was referring to in His promise to Abraham.

Be on alert as you journey on the path God has for you. The fires will burn hotter, and the tests and trials will grow harder as your faith develops.

Even when our faith is strong, we are not immune from stumbling and falling flat on our faces. Trust me, I speak from experience. Satan is not omniscient, but he has his minions, or rather demons, everywhere.

Just like any competent general in an army, Satan studies his opponent. He diligently watches and observes us. He may not tempt us to do something foolish like rob a bank, but he might plant seeds prompting us to lose our focus on God's plan.

Think back to Eve in the garden of Eden. Satan did not say to her, "Hey, Eve. Do you want to disobey God and be eternally separated from Him? Would you like to be forced to experience unbearable pain during childbirth and be thrown out of the garden forever?"

He was devious. Satan planted seeds of doubt in her mind as he questioned what God had said to Adam.

"Now the serpent was more crafty than any beast of the field which the Lord God had made. And he said to the woman. 'Indeed, has God said, "You shall not eat from any tree in the garden'?" The woman said to the serpent, 'From the fruit of the trees of the garden we may eat; but from the fruit of the tree which is in the middle of the garden, God has said, "You shall not eat from it or touch it, or you will die."' The serpent said to the woman, 'You surely will not die!'" (Genesis 3:1–4).

After we get past the fact that Eve was chatting it up with a snake, we need to recognize that this is how Satan works. He is an accuser. The devil plants seeds of doubt in our heads as he attacks our minds. He wants us to question our salvation, our relationship with Christ, and everything we do in service to Him.

During high school, I allowed the devil to plant his seeds. I had a great circle of friends. I was a superstar athlete in football and became an all-star as a basketball player. I had trophies everywhere at home in recognition of my athletic achievements. High school was one of the most enjoyable times of my life—until it wasn't.

Some of my closest friends were older than me, and I had a strong desire to graduate with them and not be left behind. I committed myself to graduate in three years instead of four.

My school workload was heavy as were the responsibilities of all my athletic endeavors. Along came the enemy to tempt me to make the wrong choices—which I did. I wasn't kicked out of "the garden," but I was denied the privilege of walking with my graduating class due to cheating.

It was humiliating, painful, and one of the worst moments of my young life. All my friends graduated on time, and I spent three months in summer school to get my diploma. I never saw any of those close friends again after that.

I share this heartbreaking story to remind us how easy it is to make the wrong choices. God has chosen us to be a vital part of His family. However, for us to be vessels that He can use, He continues to develop our faith.

Now, just because we stumble and fall does not mean that God will discard us. He is shaping us into the people He wants us to be. After my experience in high school, I learned that life doesn't have any shortcuts. Anything of value must be earned through hard work, dedication, and preparation.

More than thirty-five years have passed since those events, and I think twice (even three times) about that time before making similar choices. God is developing my Christian character and strengthening my faith. I don't need to cut corners as I put my faith and trust in Him.

Another one of my favorite people in the Bible to draw encouragement from is Joseph. His faith is an inspiration to me. God took him through several trials and tests to develop his faith as well.

He was the second youngest of twelve sons, and his father, Jacob, showed favor to him by giving him a beautiful coat of many colors. His brothers hated him with a passion (Genesis 37:4). Some of them even wanted to kill him. Eventually, they concocted a plan to get rid of their sibling.

After he was thrown in a pit by his brothers, Joseph was sold for twenty pieces of silver to traders on their way to Egypt. Can you envision being sold into slavery by your own family? Imagine Joseph's confusion at that moment.

God had blessed him with two dreams earlier in his life, indicating that someday his family would bow down to him. Instead, Joseph found himself dragged off to another country as a slave! "Now Joseph had been taken down to Egypt; and Potiphar, an Egyptian officer of Pharaoh, the captain of the bodyguard, bought him from the Ishmaelites, who had taken him down there" (Genesis 39:1).

However, God stayed by Joseph's side.

> The Lord was with Joseph, so he became a successful man. And he was in the house of his master, the Egyptian. Now his master saw that the Lord was with him and how the Lord caused all that he did to prosper in his hand. So Joseph found favor in his sight and became his personal servant; and he made him overseer over his house, and all that he owned he put in his charge. It came about that from the time he made him overseer in his house and over all that he owned, the Lord blessed the Egyptian's house on account of Joseph; thus the Lord's blessing was upon all that he owned, in the house and in the field (Genesis 39:2–5).

Well, well, well. Things were certainly looking up for Joseph. Potiphar had put him in charge of his home. He was running things like a boss. Maybe those dreams would become a reality.

Even in the midst of trials, God is always with us. Everything that takes place in our lives has a purpose. There is no randomness with God. At this point in our faith development, God is making us stronger for what lies ahead.

God will test our hearts, my friend. Repeatedly, consistently, and yet so lovingly. His desire is not to harm us but to help us become more like Christ. The tests will be painful at times, but we will reap the benefit of a stronger faith.

Even though Joseph's master thought so much of him that he put him in charge of his household, Potiphar's wife had other ideas for Joseph. She thought Joseph was handsome and wanted to have sex with him. She repeatedly pursued him to sleep with her, despite his objections. Joseph wanted to be faithful to his master and not sin against God.

Potiphar's wife attacked Joseph and accused him of trying to rape her.

He was then unjustly sent to prison, but once again, God stayed by his side. "So Joseph's master took him and put him into the jail, the place where the king's prisoners were confined; and he was there in the jail. But the Lord was with Joseph and extended kindness to him, and gave him favor in the sight of the chief jailer. The chief jailer committed to Joseph's charge all the prisoners who were in the jail, so that whatever was done there, he was responsible for it . . . The Lord was with him; and whatever he did, the Lord made to prosper" (Genesis 39:20–23).

Do you notice a theme here? Even though God is allowing Joseph to go through these painful experiences, God is *always* with him. He was prospering in the midst of these trials. As we spend difficult times in the furnace of affliction while God develops our faith, think of Joseph and what he experienced, and remember everything has a purpose.

After several years in prison and feeling as if he had been forgotten, Joseph was called before the pharaoh to interpret some dreams. After correctly interpreting the pharaoh's dreams, Joseph was made second-in-command. He was now the prime minister over all of Egypt; he had been given complete control and was one of the most powerful men in the world.

Every painful trial and test he endured had a purpose. God was preparing Joseph for his ultimate station—to be the leader of a country that would provide food for the Israelites during the famine.

This was the birth of a nation, which led to his eleven brothers traveling to Egypt and unwittingly bowing before him to request food for their families. *Shazam!* God just brought everything full circle for Joseph.

James 1:2–4 is another one of my favorite Scriptures that I memorized after my stroke. It was difficult to understand at first, but God has clarified these truths for me since then. "Consider it all joy, my brethren, when you encounter various trials, knowing that the testing of your faith produces endurance. And let endurance have its perfect result, so that you may be perfect and complete, lacking in nothing."

When I first read this verse, I was like, joy? Really, God? How can I have joy in the midst of my painful trials? But God is not asking us as Christians to joke and laugh during our tests. He is asking us to have joy, knowing that the purpose of our trials is to draw us into a deeper relationship and commitment to Christ.

"Perfect and complete" does not mean that we will be without sin; only God has no sin. But this is the ultimate level of faith that God wants to develop in us. It is the type of faith that I desire to experience on a daily basis.

EXQUISITE FAITH

"Impeccable" and "perfect" are two words that define the word "exquisite." Another word that applies when it comes to this level of faith is "refined." God has us in the refining fire, developing our faith. He desires our faith to be exceptional so that we can accomplish everything He has planned for us.

That is why we must have joy in the midst of our trials. We know God is preparing us for something, and He wants what is best for us. He promises that all things will work together for good for those who love Him and are called according to His purpose (Romans 8:28, author's paraphrase).

This Scripture is referring to working together for what God sees as good—not what we feel is good in our eyes. I'm sure Joseph did not think that being a slave and an accused rapist was good, but it was all part of God's perfect plan for his life.

Exquisite faith is living in obedience without any doubting—a faith with full confidence in God, no matter our circumstances or our feelings. When we give ourselves over to our feelings and follow them, we usually end up in trouble. It is a constant battle for me to not live according to my desires.

I am reminded of my last job interview in 2005. The interviewers asked me to tell them my greatest strength and my greatest weakness. I said that was easy. They were the same thing—my emotions.

Just as I can quickly get fired up about a project and enthusiastically hit the ground running, I can also allow those same emotions to send me into a downward spiral, wanting to cancel every account I worked on that week.

We can't live a victorious Christian life by trusting our feelings. God wants us to live our lives trusting in Him. "Now that no one is justified by the Law before God is evident; for, 'the righteous man shall live by faith'" (Galatians 3:11).

An example of exquisite faith is shown by my main man, Abraham. God had blessed him and his wife Sarah with a child as promised. However, God later gave Abraham the ultimate test. He commanded him to take his son, Isaac, up on a mountain and sacrifice him on an altar. Say what?

Abraham awakened early the next morning to do as God commanded. It was a three-day journey to the place of sacrifice, so he had plenty of time to change his mind. However, Abraham pressed forward without any doubts. He was prepared to sacrifice the heir God had promised him. After seeing Abraham's willingness to obey Him, however, God intervened and prevented Abraham from killing Isaac.

Some additional examples of exquisite faith come to mind.

I think about Queen Esther whose faith in God shone brightly in the boldness she exhibited in saving the Israelites from extermination. Her story inspires me every time I read it.

Ruth's story also moves me. Her faith in God was courageous. She is the great-grandmother of King David and is forever in the lineage of Jesus Christ, our Savior.

I recall another woman who is sometimes forgotten. She does not even have a name, or at least, it is not mentioned in the Bible. She is known as the woman with an issue of blood. This woman had been bleeding for twelve years and was unable to receive any help from physicians, despite spending all her money.

She determined that if she could get through the massive crowds following Jesus, she would be relieved of her ailment. She was not even seeking to speak with Him. Now that is faith without doubt! "For she was saying to herself, 'If I only touch His garment, I will get well.' But Jesus turning and seeing her said, 'Daughter, take courage; your faith has made you well.' At once the woman was made well" (Matthew 9:21–22).

"Your faith has made you well." Wow, those are words that I desperately want to hear from Jesus as I walk the Christian life. We must have determined courage as God develops our faith during the pain and suffering in our lives.

Part of God's purpose in our pain and suffering is developing and strengthening our faith. So as we are crossing that bridge of faith and it continues to shake violently, let's hold on tight and keep our eyes on Jesus. He is right there with us, holding our hands, helping our faith to grow stronger every day. "In this you greatly rejoice, even though now for a little while, if necessary, you have been distressed by various trials, so that the proof of your faith, being more precious than gold which is perishable, even though tested by fire, may be found to result in praise and glory and honor at the revelation of Jesus Christ" (1 Peter 1:6–7).

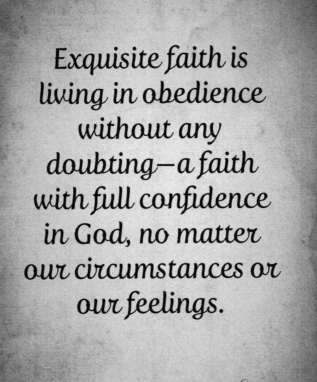

Exquisite faith is living in obedience without any doubting—a faith with full confidence in God, no matter our circumstances or our feelings.

REFINING FIRE QUESTIONS

Where are you in your faith walk? Are you still in the infancy of your Christianity, living only in saving faith, or are you progressing to a more mature level?

_____

_____

_____

What areas in your life are vulnerable to Satan and his followers as they watch your faith walk with Christ?

_____

_____

_____

Where is your level of joy in the midst of your trials? Are you living by faith in God or by your feelings?

_____

_____

_____

Fixing our eyes on Jesus, the author and perfecter of faith,
who for the joy set before Him endured the cross, despising the
shame, and has sat down at the right hand of the throne of God.
Hebrews 12:2

3

GOD USES OUR PAIN AND SUFFERING TO

DEMOLISH OUR PRIDE

While trying to find the best word for the actions God takes against our pride, I was conflicted. I didn't want the word to be too harsh, but then I realized that God cannot use us effectively until our pride is demolished.

We must experience brokenness to see the need to put our lives completely in His hands.

Joseph was a slave and imprisoned before God used him. David spent several years running and hiding in the wilderness from Saul—the king of Israel, who desperately wanted to kill him—before he could take his own seat on the throne.

It is not easy to share with you the times I have experienced God's hand destroying my pride, but I am not going to lie. I feel that God has led me to share my testimony to encourage, help, and hopefully enlighten you. He works to rid us of our pride while establishing a spirit of humility in our lives.

I'm not sure I can adequately express to you how humbling the experiences that occurred after my stroke were for me—from the initial hours to what ended up dragging into days, weeks, and then months.

I awakened to find myself wearing a catheter, strapped to a hospital bed. I could no longer sit up or even go to the bathroom on my own.

I wouldn't be rushing off to or preparing for meetings at work. I no longer needed to take my beautiful, black dream car to the car wash to keep it in pristine condition. It was just God and me in a cold, dark hospital room. My only comfort was the annoying beeping of the monitors, reminding me that I had survived the stroke.

God had tried whispering to me and even speaking to my conscience, but now, as C. S. Lewis said, He was shouting in my pain.[2] He was not shouting in anger but with compassion. God took me to the depths of brokenness, which forced me not only to hear Him but also to listen to Him.

"Thus says the Lord, 'Let not a wise man boast of his wisdom, and let not the mighty man boast of his might, let not a rich man boast of his riches; but let him who boasts boast of this, that he understands and knows Me, that I am the Lord who exercises lovingkindness, justice and righteousness on the earth, for I delight in these things,' declares the Lord" (Jeremiah 9:23–24).

Pride is an abomination to God. He will do whatever is necessary to eradicate it from our lives.

The apostle Paul wrote over half of the New Testament books that we read and study today. To keep him humble, God allowed him to relentlessly be afflicted by a thorn. (See 2 Corinthians 12:7) He was also beaten, imprisoned, almost drowned in the sea, and stoned and left for dead. (See 2 Corinthians 11:24–31) However, Paul in his humility was used by God to establish several churches and draw thousands to Christ.

Just like these men from the Bible, we will spend time in the furnace to demolish our pride. We may not spend forty years in the desert or spend days in caves running from someone who wants to kill us, but God will use whatever means necessary to get our attention and bring us to a level of brokenness as He designs in us a DNA of humility.

---

2 Lewis, *Problem of Pain*.

"The Lord is near to the brokenhearted and saves those who are crushed in spirit" (Psalm 34:18).

"The fear of the Lord is the instruction for wisdom, and before honor comes humility" (Proverbs 15:33).

"Do nothing from selfishness or empty conceit, but with humility of mind regard one another as more important than yourselves; do not merely look out for your own personal interests, but also for the interests of others. Have this attitude in yourselves which was also in Christ Jesus" (Philippians 2:3–5).

"But he gives a greater grace. Therefore it says, 'God is opposed to the proud but gives grace to the humble'" (James 4:6).

Do you want to live in opposition to God, or is your heart in alignment with His will to serve Him obediently?

Serve, surrender, and submit. Why do words like these make us feel so uncomfortable? It is about pride. For the numerous years that I ran away from God, I had no intention of surrendering my heart to Him.

A spiritual battle wages inside us as Christians—a battle between our desire to do things our own way and our desire to do things God's way. When we refuse to wait on God and His timing, moving forward without direction from Him, that is pride. It is also disobedience toward God. We might as well begin counting the days, because we'll be heading to the furnace of affliction really soon!

PITFALLS OF SELF-RELIANCE

God stated Moses was the most humble man in his day. However, he jumped ahead of God's timing when he killed an Egyptian who was mistreating one of the Israelites.

At that moment, he was forced into the wilderness of Midian to live as a shepherd for forty years. God had to break Moses and destroy his pride before He could use him to lead the children of Israel out of captivity in Egypt.

God cannot use us fully for His glory until our hearts are tender, and our spirits are willing. It is unlikely that you will be banished to a desert or find yourself lying in a hospital, wearing a diaper as I did. Nevertheless, God will bring you to a level of brokenness that reveals your dependence on Him.

God's timing is perfect. He wants to use our lives for His glory. He is working to make our hearts humble so He can use our gifts, talents, and abilities to bring people closer to Jesus Christ.

He wanted the children of Israel to know that He had heard them call to Him during their time of slavery and that He would release them from captivity. Here is what the Lord said to Moses when He spoke to him from the burning bush, instructing him that it was time to rescue His people.

"The Lord said, 'I have surely seen the affliction of My people who are in Egypt, and have given heed to their cry because of their taskmasters, for I am aware of their sufferings. So I have come down to deliver them from the power of the Egyptians, and to bring them up from that land to a good and spacious land, to a land flowing with milk and honey'" (Exodus 3:7–8).

Consider this: Moses's self-reliance may have delayed the exodus of the Israelites. I try to avoid looking back, but it is essential to learn from past transgressions.

My selfish pride led me to rely solely on myself. I ignored God and as a result, delayed the transforming of my heart for decades. This affected me along the way, of course, but it also affected family, friends, and others I loved dearly.

"Pride goes before destruction, and a haughty spirit before stumbling. It is better to be humble in spirit with the lowly than to divide the spoil with the proud" (Proverbs 16:18–19).

"The fear of the Lord is the instruction for wisdom, and before honor comes humility" (Proverbs 15:33).

When we think we know better than God and think that His instructions don't make sense, we need to resist the urge to rely on our own interpretations of what is right. Otherwise, we will endure painful consequences. I guarantee it!

Jumping ahead of God's timing and His will also reveals a lack of trust in Him. How can we not trust the One who shed His blood for us on the cross?

My insistence on self-reliance became evident during my engagement. Unfortunately, I had repeatedly ignored God's prompting at that time. My beautiful fiancée offered poignant and soft-spoken words: "You are supposed to be the leader, a man of God to lead both of us."

My decision to rely solely on myself to guide my life and to disregard God and the words of wisdom he sent to me through others led to a litany of broken and unfulfilled relationships.

A year after our engagement, my fiancée and I broke up. It was the lowest point of my life until suffering through my stroke twenty-two years later. Yet even in my gut-wrenching pain, I still refused to turn to God, and I relied only on myself.

Here is an example of when prideful sin isn't as easy to spot but still leads to unpleasant consequences. Let's say you drive on a road that has a sign warning you about high water at times. One day, you decide that your car is special, and despite the warning signs and the constant rain for the past few days, you choose to drive on that road, thinking the water cannot be that deep.

Within minutes, you realize that your car is no longer hugging the road as you hear the sound of rushing water gurgling inside your vehicle. Before you know it, you are careening down the street. You have lost control, and water starts rising quickly inside your car.

All of a sudden, you can no longer feel the gas and brake pedals at your feet because of the ice-cold water. The steering wheel has become useless, and you are helpless. You cry out to God, "Lord, help me!" Without warning, your car comes to an abrupt stop. *Bang!*

The airbag deploys, and you peer out the window, completely frazzled. Your car has been stopped by a crumpled warning sign that reads, "High Water Crossing."

Self-reliance: 1; You: 0.

How likely do you think you will be to venture down that street on a rainy day ever again? Probably not very likely, and you may find another route to travel, even on sunny days! I believe you would be committed to paying attention to the warning signs, don't you?

Now, decades after my canceled wedding, God has become my first love. I realize my need for Him every day. He is the first person I speak with in the morning and the One I love to talk with as my head hits the pillow at night. I thank Him daily for the continued healing of both my physical and my emotional pain. I desire to bring people closer to the Savior, whom I love. He has brought me to a place of complete dependence on Him.

Humility does not require that we walk around with our heads hung in shame. No, God instructs us to have joy in the midst of our trials and tribulation (James 1:2). Our testimony as Christians is to shine brightly as we go through painful experiences while continuing to draw others to Christ.

The Lord is near to
the brokenhearted
and saves those who
are crushed in spirit.

Psalm 34:18

REFINING FIRE QUESTIONS

What areas in your life regarding pride need immediate attention? Impatience? Lack of trust? List them here, and pray about them right now.

_____

_____

_____

Do you have someone in your life who helps keep you humble? Who is this person, and are you in constant contact with him or her to prevent you from puffing up?

_____

_____

_____

In what ways are you willing to truly humble yourself so that you can be used effectively as a vessel for God? If you do not humble yourself, what do you think is on the horizon for you?

_____

_____

_____

When pride comes, then comes dishonor,
but with the humble is wisdom.

Proverbs 11:2

4

GOD USES OUR PAIN AND SUFFERING TO

DETERMINE OUR PATHS

Even though the breakup with my fiancée was an agonizing experience that left me with emotional scars for years, I didn't get on the right path until more than twenty-five years later.

Please hear me on this: God is trying to speak to us through our pain. The paths we follow to reach God's intended purpose are up to us. Are we willing to humble ourselves and be used by the Lord, or do we shake our fists in anger and curse Him in our pain?

One of the most well-known stories of pain and suffering in the Bible is the story of Job. Job loved the Lord with all his heart and lived a life that was pleasing to Him.

God blessed Job with ten children, and he was one of the wealthiest men of his time. God had blessed him in abundance. Look how proud God was of Job as He questioned Satan. "The Lord said to Satan, 'From where do you come?' Then Satan answered the Lord and said, 'From roaming about on the earth and walking around on it.' The Lord said to Satan, 'Have you considered my servant Job? For there is no one like him on the earth, a blameless and upright man, fearing God and turning away from evil'" (Job 1:7–8).

Satan scoffed at the Lord's statement. He felt that because Job was so well-off and God had prospered everything in Job's life that of course, he behaved in a godly manner.

Unbeknownst to Job, God's faith in him was so staunch that He gave Satan permission to do anything to Job except kill him. Satan jumped at the opportunity to prove that God's faith was misplaced. He believed Job would curse God if everything was taken away from him.

Satan killed all ten of his children. Then he destroyed some of Job's livestock and allowed the rest to be stolen. Job lost everything. If that were not bad enough, Satan then attacked Job's health, ravaging him with boils all over his body. (On multiple occasions since my stroke, I have experienced the searing pain of a single boil—I cannot imagine being covered with them from head to toe like Job was.)

Even his wife implored him to turn away from God! Look at their conversation as Job sat in a pile of ashes, scraping his boils. "Then his wife said to him, 'Do you still hold fast to your integrity? Curse God and die!' But he said to her, 'You speak as one of the foolish women speaks. Shall we indeed accept good from God and not accept adversity?' In all this Job did not sin with his lips" (Job 2:9–10).

In reviewing some of the painful moments of my life, I see the many times I repeatedly chose the wrong path.

God desires to transform us in the midst of our pain. He's in the process of purifying us from habitual sin, and we are covered in the shed blood of Jesus Christ. He is developing humility within us, along with a servant spirit, and He wants to transform how we behave and think. "Therefore I urge you, brethren, by the mercies of God to present your bodies a living and holy sacrifice, acceptable to God, which is your spiritual service of worship. And do not be conformed to this world, but be transformed by the renewing of your mind, so that you may prove what the will of God is, that which is good and acceptable and perfect" (Romans 12:1–2).

As I've learned the hard way, God does not bless us with the gift of salvation so that we can live any way we see fit. He gave me several warning signs throughout my life that I was on the wrong path.

We are unique and have been chosen by God to bring Him glory and to draw people to Christ. So we must continually ask ourselves if we are doing exactly that with our lives.

If so, are we serving Him for the right reasons? Being a Christian is so much more than just a stay-out-of-hell card.

Go back and look at some of those sneaky sins I mentioned in chapter 1. God sees all and knows all, so we need to be honest with ourselves. Otherwise, we might suffer the consequences of some painful time in the furnace.

> You are the salt of the earth; but if the salt has become tasteless how can it be made salty again? It is no longer good for anything except to be thrown out and trampled under foot by men. You are the light of the world. A city set on a hill cannot be hidden; nor does anyone light a lamp and put it under a basket, but on a lampstand, and it gives light to all who are in the house. Let your light shine before men in such a way that they may see your good works and glorify your Father who is in Heaven (Matthew 5:13–16).

I admit that at the time of my stroke, almost thirty-eight years after I asked Christ to come into my heart, my salt had become pretty flavorless. My light was shrouded in sin, and I was in no way bringing glory to God.

Just as David did, I continually ask God to search me and reveal any sin in my life.

SIN IS NOT THE ONLY REASON WE EXPERIENCE PAIN AND SUFFERING

Here are several other possible causes of pain and suffering in our lives for us to consider.

ATTACKS FROM SATAN

In December of 2016, I published a book titled *Unleash the Power of Prayer in Your Life*. Only a few days after publication, I was struck by extremely painful, messy, and bloody health issues that prevented me from doing my scheduled book marketing and promoting for months.

I couldn't even be at my computer to write. I visited several doctors, hoping someone could diagnose me. The doctors had nothing more than guesses and suppositions; each doctor seemed as confused by what was taking place within my body as the next one. I was beyond perplexed, suffering greatly, and utterly discouraged.

I received a message on my website during this time from a sister in Christ. She mentioned that she knew as soon as she heard I was publishing a book on the power of prayer that I would be a target for Satan. She reminded me to arm myself in the armor of God (Ephesians 6:11) every day and prepare myself for spiritual warfare, something that I now take to heart daily.

After suffering for three-and-a-half months, an MRI revealed a possible cause of the problem. I still have to manage the pain, because according to my surgeon, it is not fixable; surgery would only lead to additional issues.

Today, I am so thankful that God is healing my body without medications. I still experience pain but not to a degree that prevents me from writing about my Savior. Praise God!

Satan's plans of attack have not changed much since the fall of Adam and Eve. Why would he switch from what works? Know this, my sister or brother in Christ: As we seek to live for God, we will experience painful trials and tribulations. Read how the apostle Paul warns his young protégé, Timothy, about suffering. "Indeed, all who desire to live godly in Christ Jesus will be persecuted" (2 Timothy 3:12).

Jesus also warned His disciples that after His death and ascension to heaven that they would experience difficult trials. "These things I have spoken to you, so that in Me you may have peace. In the world you will have tribulation but take courage; I have overcome the world" (John 16:33).

Choosing the right path in our own strength can be daunting when extreme difficulties litter the road. Jesus Christ has made the way for us to follow Him with determined courage.

OUR INHERENTLY SINFUL NATURE

Since the fall of Adam and Eve, sin has infected humanity. So, unfortunately, it is natural for people to sin.

The unexpected death of a loved one is one of the most painful experiences that can take place in our lives. I attended the funeral of my baby niece after one of my sisters had a daughter who was stillborn. The church ceremony was beautiful, but I struggled mightily to stand at the gravesite and watch my niece's tiny, pink casket be lowered into the ground. I had to walk away and listen to the pastor's prayer from a distance. No reason for this loss. Just unexplainable heart-wrenching pain.

Think back to Job; he had no earthly idea he was a pawn in the conflict taking place between God and Satan in the spiritual realm. However, look at the path he chose when he was supposedly encouraged and chastised by his so-called friends. "But He knows the way I take; When He has tried me, I shall come forth as gold. My foot has held fast to His path; I have kept His way and not turned aside. I have not departed from the command of His lips; I have treasured the word of His mouth more than my necessary food" (Job 23:10–12).

Will we choose the same path as Job in the midst of our pain, or will we become angry and rebel against God?

SELF-INFLICTED PAIN

I had plenty of time for God to reveal this to me while I was lying in that hospital bed. I remembered all the earlier warnings from doctors on my occasional visits. I thought about the unhealthy eating and sleep habits I had developed over the years leading up to my stroke.

The sneaky sins of pride and selfishness had come home to reap a painful and devastating harvest. However, God chose not to end my life on that day in July, and I am thankful that He is restoring my physical health and my relationship with Him. His purpose for me is still at work.

In the Bible, Samson serves as a great example of self-inflicted pain. He was the strongest man ever created, destined by God to be a Nazirite and deliver Israel from the hand of the Philistines (Judges 13:5).

He wasted the blessing of incredible strength from God with his disobedient disposition and lustful heart. His desire to be with a beautiful but also deceitful Philistine woman named Delilah led to his ultimate downfall.

Delilah tricked Samson into allowing her to shave the long locks of hair on his head, which resulted in the loss of every ounce of his God-given strength. "She said, 'The Philistines are upon, you, Samson!' And he awoke from his sleep and said, 'I will go out as at other times and shake myself free.' *But he did not know that the Lord had departed from him*" (Judges 16:20, emphasis added).

At his self-inflicted death, Samson could finally accomplish the Lord's will for his life. We have to guard ourselves so that our pain is not self-induced. God might allow us to walk that treacherous path if we are determined to do things our own way.

DISCIPLINE OR INSTRUCTION

Outside of sin, here is another reason and possible cause for our pain and suffering.

When I speak of discipline, I am not referring to the discipline that comes as punishment for doing something wrong. I'm referring to training that involves instruction, a discipline that brings about change. Sometimes God may allow a particular trial to take place to help us in our relationship with Him.

> For consider Him who has endured such hostility by sinners against Himself, so that you will not grow weary and lose heart. You have not yet resisted to the point of shedding blood in your striving against sin; and you have forgotten the exhortation which is addressed to you as sons, *My son, do not regard lightly the discipline of the Lord, nor faint when you are reproved by Him; for those whom the Lord loves He disciplines, and scourges every son whom He receives.* It is for discipline that you endure; God deals with you as with sons; for what son is there whom his father does not discipline? But if you are without discipline, of which all have become partakers, then you are illegitimate children and not sons . . . . For they disciplined us for a short time as seemed best to them, *but He disciplines us for our good, so that we may share His holiness. All discipline for the moment seems not to be joyful, but sorrowful; yet to those who have been trained by it, afterwards it yields the peaceful fruit of righteousness.* Therefore, strengthen the hands that are weak and the knees that are feeble (Hebrews 12:3–8, 10–12, emphasis added).

God is perfect, God is just, and God is love. God has welcomed you into His family. His desire is for you to live an abundant life (John 10:10, author's paraphrase).

We should ask ourselves if we are seeking God wholeheartedly in the midst of our pain. God desires an intimate relationship with us. We cannot casually date God or fool around with Him when it's convenient. He wants our heart wholly committed to Him.

ROAD MAP FOR THE RIGHT PATH

Here are three best practices to help you stay on the path that God intends for you to follow.

MEDITATE ON THE PROMISES OF GOD

Ponder. Deliberate. Reflect. Choose whichever word resonates with you the most, and apply it to your life. We cannot meditate on God's Word once in a while or when we happen to have the time. We must make this a daily practice in our lives.

When I read His Word, I use a study Bible when possible. I'm desperate to understand what the Lord has to say to me. If I read something and don't understand it, I check the study Bible notes for reference and a better understanding. That is usually when the light bulb comes on and the Scripture makes sense.

As you read the Spirit-infused words of God, ask Him, "What do You want to teach me, Lord?" Ask God for the wisdom to understand His Scriptures of truth. He promises He will give it to you freely (James 1:5, author's paraphrase).

Start small if you must, but start. Spend intentional time in God's Word! Dive into your Bible with abandon, and immerse yourself in the comforting promises of God, who loves you unconditionally.

Here are some of my favorite life Scripture verses overflowing with incredible assurances from our Father. "Trust in the Lord with all your heart and do not lean on your own understanding. In all your ways acknowledge

Him, and He will make your paths straight. Do not be wise in your own eyes; fear the Lord and turn away from evil. It will be healing to your body and refreshment to your bones" (Proverbs 3:5–8).

Growing up, I'd glance at the first two verses so I could tell my parents that I had read my Bible. However, this entire passage is filled with promises from God. Now, I recite these verses to myself many times, especially during prayers.

God will make our paths straight when we recognize His authority in our lives and the world around us. He is a sovereign God. This Scripture also gives promises of healing and comfort, something we need in the midst of our pain and suffering.

Memorization is an active form of meditating on God's Word. Having Bible scriptures ready for any situation can help keep us on the path that God desires.

"How can a young man keep his way pure? By keeping it according to your Word. *With all my heart I have sought You*; do not let me wander from Your commandments. Your word I have treasured in my heart, that I might not sin against You . . . . *I will meditate on Your precepts* and regard Your ways. *I shall delight in Your statutes; I shall not forget Your Word*" (Psalm 119:9–11, 15–16, emphasis added).

APPLICATION

Meditation is just the beginning. If we desire to maintain the correct course and minimize our time in the furnace, we must apply the instructions from God's Word to our lives.

> Putting aside all filthiness and all that remains of wicked-ness, *in humility receive the word implanted, which is able to save your souls. But prove yourselves doers of the word, and not merely hearers who delude themselves.* For if anyone is a hearer of the word and not a doer, he is like a man who looks at his

natural face in the mirror; for once he has looked at himself and gone away, he has immediately forgotten what kind of person he was. *But the one who looks intently at the perfect law, the law of liberty, and abides by it, not having become a forgetful hearer but an effectual doer, this man will be blessed in what he does* (James 1:21–25, emphasis added).

This is another incredible promise from God, a God who cannot lie (Titus 1:2). Do we want His blessings, or do we think we have a better offer? Maybe we prefer the God-like knowledge that Satan offered to Eve and her husband, Adam. How did that work out for both of them?

DEVOTION

This is the final piece of the puzzle, which will help keep us on the right path in the midst of our pain.

Are we devoted to our Savior, who died for us? Do we remember all that He suffered so that we can have a relationship with Him? "But He was pierced through for our transgressions; He was crushed for our iniquities; the chastening for our well-being fell upon Him, and by His scourging we are healed" (Isaiah 53:5).

How could we not be committed to the One who shows us such unconditional love?

Adoration. Affection. Dedication. Reverence. Worship. This is what devotion should look like in our lives and how our commitment to Christ should manifest itself—from the moment we wake each morning to the time we nod off peacefully at night. Devotion is not just on Sundays or a couple of hours each week. God wants us to show devotion toward Him every day.

We need to **m**editate on His Word, **a**pply what we read to our lives, and **d**evote ourselves to Him. We need to live MAD about—not mad at—God in the midst of our suffering. We should be madly in love with the One who saved us, living boldly in our confidence in Him and trusting that whatever

He is taking us through serves His divine purpose.

These three practices will help keep us traveling on the correct paths and implant in us the godly wisdom necessary to live fruitfully and in a way that glorifies Christ.

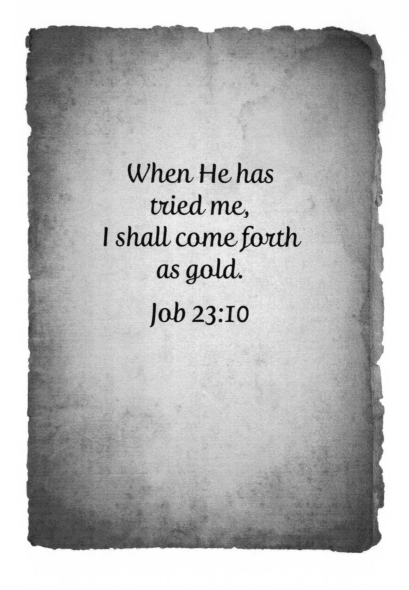

When He has
tried me,
I shall come forth
as gold.

Job 23:10

REFINING FIRE QUESTIONS

What is the primary cause of your pain and suffering? Don't be too quick to blame it on the devil. Take a long look in the mirror.

_____

_____

_____

When you are in pain, which path do you take: anger or submission? If it's anger, are you directing your anger at God? If so, why?

_____

_____

_____

Are you **MAD**ly in love with God today? In what areas are you falling short in your love for Him? Meditation, application, or devotion?

_____

_____

_____

Therefore as you have received Christ Jesus the Lord, so
walk in Him, having been firmly rooted and now being
built up in Him and established in your faith, just as you
were instructed, and overflowing with gratitude.

Colossians 2:6–7

5

GOD USES OUR PAIN AND SUFFERING TO

DEMONSTRATE HIS GRACE

Different types of pain exist for various amounts of time. God in His infinite wisdom knows exactly how long and to what extent we should experience pain. He is in complete control regarding the intensity of our suffering. God's grace—His undeserved favor—is never in short supply for His children.

God always extends His grace to us, particularly in the moments before He welcomes us into His family. He also vividly demonstrates His grace in the midst of our pain and suffering.

Moses committed murder, and was forced to leave family and everything familiar. He lived in the desert for forty years before God chose him to lead the nation of Israel from bondage in Egypt. The apostle Paul when he was known as Saul, zealously persecuted and imprisoned Christians. However, God redeemed his soul, changed his name to Paul, and used him as a vessel to point Gentiles to Christ. The prophet Jonah disobeyed God and tried to run away from his calling. He was thrown overboard into the sea where he spent three days in the belly of a giant fish. God still used him to lead an entire city of heathens to repentance.

God's grace washes over us because He desires to use us for His glory. One phrase that you repeatedly hear from some Christians is "I am a sinner saved by grace." I can appreciate the truth of the sentiment, but take a moment to remember what we have been saved from—eternal punishment.

"And if anyone's name was not found written in the book of life, he was thrown into the lake of fire" (Revelation 20:15).

"The Son of Man will send forth His angels, and they will gather out of His kingdom all stumbling blocks, and those who commit lawlessness, and will throw them into the furnace of fire; in that place there will be weeping and gnashing of teeth. THEN THE RIGHTEOUS WILL SHINE FORTH AS THE SUN in the kingdom of their Father. He who has ears, let him hear" (Matthew 13:41–43).

We don't ever want to take for granted the grace that God continues to show us. He has saved us from eternal separation from Him, and it is foolish to test Him.

> But God, being rich in mercy, because of His great love with which He loved us, even when we were dead in our transgressions, made us alive together with Christ (by grace you have been saved), and raised us up with Him, and seated us with Him in heavenly places in Christ Jesus, *so that in the ages to come He might show the surpassing riches of His grace in kindness towards us in Christ Jesus. For by grace you have been saved through faith; and that not of yourselves, it is the gift of God, not a result of works, so that no one may boast.* For we are his workmanship, created in Christ Jesus for good works, which God prepared beforehand so that we would walk in them (Ephesians 2:4–10, emphasis added).

God blesses us with His incredible grace. We are living in its presence right now, and I am a prime example. Every year in the U.S., more than 795,000 strokes occur and approximately 140,000 people die from strokes,[3]

---

3 "Stroke Facts," Centers for Disease Control and Prevention, last updated September 6, 2017, https://www.cdc.gov/stroke/facts.htm.

but by God's grace, I survived when it happened to me. God made it possible for me to be able to read His word daily and learn from it, giving me the ability to pass on to you what He has revealed to me.

Despite the pain and suffering I still experience as a result of the stroke (many days I could easily stay in bed and cry myself to sleep because of it), God continues to show Himself faithful. Because of what He states in the Bible, I know He is molding me into the man He desires me to be so that I can glorify Him. "Do not be carried away by varied and strange teachings; *for it is good for the heart to be strengthened by grace*, not by foods, through which those who were so occupied were not benefited" (Hebrews 13:9, emphasis added).

Never forget that pain is not meant to destroy us but to develop us. **How we respond to the grace of God plays a significant role in the intensity of our pain and suffering.**

I continued to test God and the limits of His patience in the years leading up to my stroke. The verse in Hebrews gives me hope about God and His never-ending grace, and it all goes back to Adam.

> For as through one man's disobedience the many were made sinners, even so through the obedience of the One the many will be made righteous. The Law came in so that the transgression would increase; *but where sin increased, grace abounded all the more*, so that, as sin reigned in death, even so grace would reign through righteousness to eternal life through Jesus Christ our Lord. What shall we say then? Are we to continue in sin so that grace may increase? May it never be! How shall we who died to sin still live in it? Or do you not know that all of us who have been baptized into Christ Jesus have been baptized into his death? (Romans 5:19–21; 6:1–3, emphasis added).

The apostle Paul posed some hard-hitting questions in these verses. I love Paul's quotation that states as sin increased, grace abounded even more! God, in His unceasing holiness, cannot allow us to continue in sin. His desire is for us to carry ourselves more like His Son, Jesus Christ.

Another purpose of God in the midst of our pain is for us to continue maturing as Christians.

Theologian Erwin Lutzer states, "There are no shortcuts to spiritual maturity. It takes time to be holy."[4] Now, before we get too get upset and state how grown up we are, remember the following: when we accept Christ into our hearts at any age, we're born again (John 3:3).

We are babes in Christ. God desires to help foster our spiritual growth, and sometimes that can bring about growing pains.

For the parents out there, do you remember your children's "terrible twos" or trying teenage years?

I'm sure you wondered many times how to handle certain situations with your children; am I right? I am not a parent, but I have eleven nephews and nieces and have seen glimpses of the terrible twos. Seeing that type of behavior reminded me why I remained single. (I'm joking, of course; I love all of them dearly. They are precious gifts from God.)

I have witnessed moments of my siblings' grace toward their children at the height of their temperamental behaviors. My siblings didn't throw in the towel, giving up on their children.

They desire to instruct, mold, and develop their children in the way God wants to instruct each of us. Training children is not always an easy thing to do, but it is necessary. God grants us His undeserved grace as He continues instructing, molding, and developing us. Trust me; God has no desire for us to remain at the terrible twos stage of spiritual maturity. Read what the author of the book of Hebrews wrote to the believers of that time. "For though by this time you ought to be teachers, you have need again for someone to teach you the elementary principles of the oracles of God, and you have come to need milk and not solid food. For everyone who partakes only of

---

4 Erwin W. Lutzer , *Failure: The Back Door to Success,* (Chicago: Moody Publishers, 1975, 2016) 96.

milk is not accustomed to the word of righteousness, for he is an infant. But solid food is for the mature, who because of practice have their senses trained to discern good and evil" (Hebrews 5:12–14).

This scripture is a reminder of our need to go from saving faith in God to maturing in our salvation. Unless we desire to become flavorless Christians, we must make growing in Christ a priority. God is always there to guide us to full maturity in Him. Some seasons of development may be more painful than others, but His purpose and plan is for our good and His glory.

So, regardless of where we are in the spiritual maturity timeline—the infant stage, the puberty stage, living in the landmine of a rebellious teenager, or a spiritually maturing adult—we can't get stuck in the know-it-all stage.

We shouldn't give in to fear and doubt as we mature; we shouldn't think that we are "over the hill" and that God can no longer use us. I had just turned forty-six years old when I recommitted my life to Christ at First Baptist Church in Dallas. Even if you are advanced in age and feel you are closer to the end of your life than the beginning, God has a plan and a purpose for your life.

The question we need to ask ourselves is whether we are willing to trust His plan.

BENEFITS OF GOD'S GRACE

Based on my own experiences and the revelations from God through Scripture, I want to share some of the irreplaceable benefits of God's grace with you. Think about your children or your time as a child in how this relates to your spiritual growth.

LEARNING

God desires for us to understand so much and wants to teach us in the midst of our trials. So where can we get this training and instruction? In His word.

It is the ultimate study guide for our lives. Sixty-six Holy Spirit–infused books by forty God-chosen authors are available to give us the instruction we need. "All Scripture is inspired by God and profitable for teaching, for reproof, for correction, for training in righteousness; so that the man of God may be adequate, equipped for every good work" (2 Timothy 3:16–17).

Would you send your young child out to apply for work at a factory, grocery store, or a coffee shop? No, because he or she is not equipped to handle everything required in those roles. So let me ask you this: When raising your children (or even your pets if you have no children), do you let them run around, doing whatever they want, with the idea that that they will figure out everything in life? I certainly hope not.

Whichever stage our spiritual life is in, God is preparing us for the role He has planned for us—a plan He began to shape from the moment we were born (Romans 8:29). This preparation involves difficult, trying, and persistent pain at times.

When I was fourteen years old, I experienced some pain in my preparation. Every Wednesday morning at school, we would meet in the sanctuary for a short chapel service before classes started. The boys were required to wear a sports coat or blazer to the service.

A few of the upperclassmen football players would wear their letterman football jackets instead. I was only a freshman and did not have a letterman jacket, but I owned a cool black leather jacket that I wanted to wear on this particular day.

My mother had other ideas, however. She inquired why I had that jacket on and requested that I return to my room to get a sport coat instead. *Sport coat? The chapel is not a church. I am going to school. I don't need a stupid sport coat!* These thoughts screamed in my mind as I stormed back to my room to follow my mother's instructions.

But then I had a brilliant idea. I would put on the sports coat now and change when I got to school—Mom would never be the wiser. I was a genius! I pulled out the coat from the closet and begrudgingly put it on before

I stuffed my black leather jacket into my gym bag.

The drive to school seemed to take longer than usual. Mom pulled into the parking lot and watched as we exited the car. I did not kiss her goodbye that morning. I'd show her. Instead of heading to the chapel, I made a bee-line for the gymnasium and bounded joyfully toward the locker room for the "great jacket switch."

I excitedly turned the dial on my locker. Once opened, I hastily took off the sports coat and shoved it into its hiding place with disdain. Next I pulled out my beautiful leather jacket from my bag, and as I put it on, I checked myself out in the mirror. I was looking good. Those seniors had nothing on me. I was a freshman on the varsity football and basketball teams. I was feeling myself—I was too cool for school!

I closed my locker and headed out of the locker room with the glow of my foolish pride. As I turned the corner, guess who waited at the end of the hall—my mother. She gently whispered seven words I will never forget as long as I live: "I'll see you when you get home." She didn't yell; she wasn't outwardly angry or hysterical. She calmly stated those words, turned around, and left the gymnasium.

I had such an uneasy feeling in the pit of my stomach. I felt miserable all day long, crestfallen. My wave of joy had come crashing down, damaging everything in its path. I returned to my locker and got my sports coat.

What had I done? All this for a jacket that I would wear for only thirty minutes at most that day. My mother had shown me grace in spite of the disappointment evident on her face that morning.

I tried to delay the inevitable and avoided going home when school was out that afternoon. I wanted to run away and hide. Finally, after I was sure everyone had been picked up, I began walking the long journey home.

My feet were on fire as I dragged them up to our front door. The pit in my stomach had morphed into the Grand Canyon. I walked toward my room. Mother was calm and still did not yell. She was glad I was safe and had made it home.

I took my time eating dinner because I knew my consequences would soon be revealed. Within hours, my backside would be hotter than my feet were on that long walk home!

I returned to my room to do my homework; my mother had laid out the thinnest pair of pajamas for me to put on. It was not bedtime, but she wanted to make sure that my backside informed my brain of the lesson I was supposed to learn; it was of little use to use the rod of instruction through a pair of thick blue jeans. She wanted me to remember this instruction. You can see that thirty-eight years later, it worked. I have not forgotten.

I share this story with you to remind you of this: Sometimes the things we experience or that God asks of us will make no sense at all. God requires that we trust Him and believe that everything taking place in our lives happens with His approval.

Everything—I mean everything—has a purpose. God is *never* caught off guard or surprised by the events in our lives. That brings me to the second benefit of God's grace.

LOVING

Never forget how much God loves us. He created us, formed us in the womb, and grows us up in Him. **God is love.** As His children, Christ-like love should be evident to everyone in our lives.

We must show this Christ-like love to our spouses, children, siblings, extended family, friends, and especially the strangers who pass through our lives every day. A love like His is what God wants to cultivate in our hearts. "So, as those who have been chosen of God, holy and beloved, put on a heart of compassion, kindness, humility, gentleness, and patience; bearing with one another, and forgiving each other, whoever has a complaint against anyone; just as the Lord forgave you, so also should you. *Beyond all these things put on love*, which is the perfect bond of unity" (Colossians 3:12–14, emphasis added).

Put on love: these words of instruction command us to love others. Why is love so important in our daily walk? These words from God's textbook can give us some insight.

"Therefore be imitators of God, as beloved children; and walk in love, just as Christ also loved you and gave Himself up for us, an offering and a sacrifice to God as a fragrant aroma" (Ephesians 5:1–2).

"Beloved, let us love one another, for love is from God; and everyone who loves is born of God and knows God. The one who does not love does not know God, for God is love" (1 John 4:7–8).

Here's a prayer from Jesus to His heavenly Father for his children. "O righteous Father, although the world has not known You, yet I have known You; and these have known that You sent Me; and I have made Your name known to them, and will make it known, so that the love with which You loved Me may be in them, and I in them" (John 17:25–26).

Jesus' prayer was that His love would be evident in you and me. A Christ-like love should be pumping in our hearts, coursing through our veins, and oozing out to everyone we come in contact with.

Here is the final benefit of God's grace that I want to share with you. It is vital to fulfilling God's purpose in our lives.

LIVING

God does not scoop us up to heaven in a chariot of fire the minute we accept Christ as our Savior. His grace has given us the opportunity to live for Him victoriously! God saved us, and now we are living within His grace. Our lives should bring glory to Him—not just on Sundays at church but every day. "Let your light shine before men in such a way that they may see your good works, and glorify your Father who is in heaven" (Matthew 5:16).

The first part of this next Scripture passage became my mission statement after I committed to creating my website and publishing my writing. *"So that you will walk in a manner worthy of the Lord, to please Him in all respects, bearing fruit in every good work and increasing in the knowledge of God;* strengthened with all power, according to his glorious might, for the attaining of all steadfastness and patience; joyously giving thanks to the Father, who has qualified us to share in the inheritance of the saints in Light" (Colossians 1:10–12, emphasis added).

Are we living in a way that glorifies God? What does the spiritual fruit look like in our lives? Is our fruit nourishing, encouraging, and inspiring others? Is it beautiful, growing, and pleasing to the eyes of our Savior?

It's my hope and prayer that we commit to not taking advantage of God's amazing grace—that we do not disrespect or ignore what He wants to do in our lives in the midst of trials and tribulations. As the apostle Paul stated, "May it never be!" (See Romans 6:1–2 NASB).

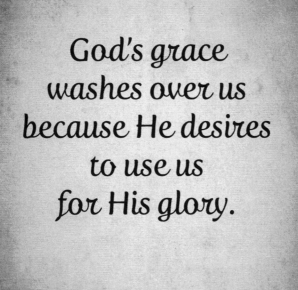

God's grace
washes over us
because He desires
to use us
for His glory.

REFINING FIRE QUESTIONS

How have you experienced God's grace in your life? Jot down a few of the ways here. Thank Him for His grace.

_____

_____

_____

As you look at your spiritual growth right now, what type of food are you feasting on currently? In what ways can you enhance your growth as a Christian?

_____

_____

_____

What does the fruit look like in your spiritual garden? What do people see in your life?

_____

_____

_____

And the grace of our Lord was more than abundant, with
the faith and love which are found in Christ Jesus.
1 Timothy 1:14

Concerning this I implored the Lord three times that
it might leave me. And He has said to me, "My grace is
sufficient for you, for power is perfected in weakness."
Most gladly, therefore, I will rather boast about my
weaknesses, so that the power of Christ may dwell in me.
2 Corinthians 12:8–9

6

GOD USES OUR PAIN AND SUFFERING TO

DISPLAY HIS LOVE

It was one of the most unforgettable times I was disciplined growing up—the mischief with my leather jacket and the consequences that resulted in an extremely sore bottom. One thing my mother said to me during my discipline was, "This is hurting me more than it is hurting you."

Have you ever heard that phrase before? At the time of my discipline, I believed it was just something from the parents' code of conduct handbook—something parents are required to say to try to ease the pain.

However, when parents have genuine love for a child, they derive no pleasure while inflicting the pain of discipline on their flesh and blood. Likewise, we are children of God, and His love for us is unconditional. As beloved members of His family, we will experience times when He uses the pain to achieve His purpose.

In the midst of our painful trials, we must always remember God's unyielding love. He gave His only Son as a sacrifice for our sins. So as we desire to live in exquisite faith, we trust in Him, not our feelings. We can't forget God's love, and we should seek refuge in the comfort of His bosom.

"And not only this, but we also exult in our tribulations, knowing that tribulation brings about perseverance; and perseverance, proven character; and proven character, hope; and hope does not disappoint, *because the love of God has been poured out within our hearts* through the Holy Spirit who was given to us" (Romans 5:3–5, emphasis added).

One of the most recognized passages of the Bible is Psalm 23, which refers to the Lord as our shepherd. He is our shepherd, and we are His sheep—sheep that He was willing to lay down His life for so that we could have eternal life with Him.

Did you know that sheep are not among the brightest of species in the animal kingdom? This is why they need a shepherd—they get lost easily and tend to wander away from the flock without giving it a second thought. Sheep are defenseless animals as well. They have no claws or sharp teeth and must rely entirely on the loving care of the shepherd.

God knows His children better than we know ourselves because He created each one of us. However, sometimes He must use the crook on the end of His staff to keep us on our designated path.

When we wander from God's loving presence, we encounter times of pain, fear, and even confusion. However, God in His unconditional love uses these painful circumstances to reinforce our dependence on Him. In verse four of Psalm 23, David states, "Even though I walk through the valley of the shadow of death, I will fear no evil for You are with me; Your rod and your staff, they comfort me."

I'm not sure how much comfort I felt from the "rod" when I was four-teen, but despite the pain, I was learning the importance of obedience and not giving in to the peer pressure of being like everyone else.

I love this quote from Charles "Chuck" Swindoll. He is a Christian pastor, author, and Bible teacher on his radio program, *Insight for Living*.

> As God's sheep, we are sometimes led by Him into the valley of darkness, where there is fear, danger, uncertainty, and the unexpected. He knows the only way we can reach higher places of Christian experience and maturity is not

on the playground of prosperity but in the schoolroom of suffering. Along those dark, narrow, pinching valleys of difficulty we learn volumes. We keep our courage because our Shepherd is leading the way.[5]

It is such a shame how easily we can ignore God's instructions when things are going well. Adam and Eve had everything they could ever want, but still they wanted more, which cost them dearly.

What started in the garden demonstrates the magnitude of God's indescribable, unbelievable, and unconditional love. His love toward us was more than evident when He sacrificed His only Son, Jesus, so that we may have the opportunity to foster an intimate relationship with Him and live with Him for eternity.

"My sheep hear My voice, and I know them, and they follow Me; and I give eternal life to them, and they will never perish; and no one will snatch them out of My hand. My Father, who has given them to Me, is greater than all; and no one is able to snatch them out of the Father's hand. I and the Father are one" (John 10:27–30).

What an inspiring promise from our Savior and shepherd, Jesus Christ. Remember His promises in the midst of your trials, pain, and suffering.

"Many are the sorrows of the wicked, *but he who trusts in the LORD, lovingkindness shall surround him.* Be glad in the Lord and rejoice, you righteous ones; and shout for joy, all you who are upright in heart" (Psalm 32:10–11, emphasis added).

"He has not dealt with us according to our sins, nor rewarded us according to our iniquities. For as high as the heavens are above the earth, *so great is His lovingkindness toward those who love Him*"(Psalm 103:10–11, emphasis added).

I hope you understand how far reaching God's love truly is—it is uncon-

---

5 Charles R. Swindoll, *Living the Psalms: Encouragement for the Daily Grind*, (Brentwood: Worthy Publishing, 2012).

ditional. It is easy to let past experiences or our ideas of love adversely affect how we view the concept. As a teenager not seeking the Lord, my view of love was based on secular love songs, movies, and television shows that I'd try to sneak samples of when I could.

In the years following the breakup with my fiancée, I had several unsuccessful relationships with women who did not know Christ. My version of love continued to line up with the worldly view of romantic love, and Christ was nowhere to be found.

In the painful, isolated nights in the hospital after my stroke, I began to realize the true nature of God's love. Because of the love He has shown me, I now write to you. I want you to experience His love in every situation.

Definite. Complete. Unlimited. These are just a few of the words that define unconditional. *God's love has no strings attached.* "See how great a love the Father has bestowed on us, that we would be called the children of God; and such we are" (1 John 3:1).

Talking about God's love has been one of the most challenging of all the chapters in creating this book. Even though I feel the love of God and experience His undeserved grace and mercy, His unconditional love is hard to grasp and wrap my head around at times.

As I dove deeper into God's Word, searching for answers and revelations to share with you, God showed Himself faithful in bringing me back to this passage of Scripture that I studied in a Sunday school class a few months ago. Read the apostle Paul's prayer to the Christians at the church in Ephesus.

> For this reason I bow my knees before the Father, from whom every family in heaven and earth derives its name, that He would grant you, according to the riches of His glory, to be strengthened with power through his Spirit in the inner man, so that Christ may dwell in your hearts through faith, *and that you being rooted and grounded in love, may be able to comprehend with all the saints what is the breadth and length and height and depth, and to know the love of Christ*

which surpasses knowledge, that you may be filled up to all the fullness of God (Ephesians 3:14–19, emphasis added).

Paul wants us to understand the vastness of God's incredible and unconditional love, and reading this passage of Scripture gives me comfort. There is nowhere the love of God cannot reach us in the midst of our pain and suffering.

After my stroke, I had to leave both the hospital and the rehab facility. The limits of my insurance played a considerable role. I believe in my heart that those events, though difficult, happened for a reason. Because of the suddenness of those events, I lived at my parents' home while I recovered.

God had spoken to me during my recovery, and I desired to know as much about Him as possible. I listened to Christian radio and sought pastors on television who were teaching from God's Word. If I did not feel that the pastor was teaching from the Bible, I'd move on in my search.

One of the pastors who drew me in with his Biblical teaching, humble spirit, and Christ-like attitude was Dr. Charles F. Stanley. He is the senior pastor of First Baptist Church in Atlanta, Georgia. He is also a renowned Bible teacher and the founder and president of InTouch Ministries.

During one of my daily devotions, I read a book he had written many years ago, which resonated with me. Recently, a brother in Christ recommended I again read that same book when I told him I was writing about pain and suffering. It was God's way of leading me to share His thoughts with you.

The title of his book is *The Blessings in the Brokenness: Why God Allows Us to Go through Hard Times.* Read what Dr. Stanley wrote twenty plus years ago about God's love.

> The motivation behind everything that God does in our lives and everything He allows in our lives is love. God does not allow brokenness in our lives because He is ruthless, cruel, heartless, or without compassion. No! To the contrary. God sees the full potential for our lives, and

He deeply desires an intimate, loving spiritual relationship with us. He wants to bring about our best, and for us to experience him in the fullness of His love, wisdom, power, strength, and goodness. He allows brokenness in our lives in order to bring about a blessing.[6]

Friend, you may not feel the effects of God's love in the midst of your pain and suffering. However, there is so much more to this than what you feel in your fallen flesh. Whether you believe it or not, God has a specific purpose and plan for you. Your time spent in the furnace of affliction is an effort to bring about God's plan.

As Dr. Stanley states in his book, "God never breaks us in anger or wrath. Rather, God moves in our lives because He loves us too much to see us continue in our sin, remain in a lukewarm spiritual state, or go unfulfilled in His purposes for our lives. God loves us too much to see us remain as we are."[7]

I have a strong desire to continue learning all about God as I seek to glorify and live for Him. I'm thankful that my life has become more focused on getting spiritual food than actual food. (My appetite for the latter put me in the hospital all those years ago.)

An exhilaration rushes over me that makes me so excited to share what God revealed—whether it be with a close friend or in an article on my website.

Read this passage from God's Word; I hope it will encourage your heart both when you're hurting and every day.

"For the love of Christ controls us, having concluded this, that one died for all, therefore all died; and He died for all, so that they who live might no longer live for themselves, but for Him who died and rose again on their behalf" (2 Corinthians 5:14–15).

---

6 Charles F. Stanley, *The Blessings of Brokenness, Why God Allows Us to Go Through Hard Times* (Grand Rapids: Zondervan, 1997) 17–18.
7 Stanley, *The Blessings of Brokenness*, 18.

The apostle Paul wanted to impress on the Christians at the church of Corinth how the love of Jesus Christ should be their motivation to change. Paul was no longer persecuting and imprisoning Christians. His desire was for their spiritual well-being and to help them improve their relationships with Christ.

Only a supernatural love transforms hearts and renews the minds of so many. God's love is everlasting, and yes, it can be painful at times, but His love comforts us when we are hurting. God has blessed me with the opportunity to live out this next passage of Scripture since my stroke.

"Blessed be the God and Father of our Lord Jesus Christ, the Father of mercies and the God of all comfort, who comforts us in all our affliction so that we will be able to comfort those who are in any affliction with the comfort with which we ourselves are comforted by God. For just as the sufferings are ours in abundance, so also our comfort is abundant through Christ" (2 Corinthians 1:3–5).

As I lay in that hospital bed many years ago, talking and listening to God, I had no idea that He would use the experience to begin a ministry for Him. When He put it on my heart to share my testimony of faith through my writing, I was both anxious and excited, wanting to encourage and offer hope to those who were hurting.

When I receive emails from people who are experiencing pain or whose family members have been affected by a stroke, I look toward the heavens and thank God for the confirmation that I am doing His will. I ask Him to give me the right words of encouragement and wisdom drawn from the fountain of His holy Word.

Only a God who loves His children unconditionally does things like that. God is concerned about every aspect of our lives. Have you relinquished your whole life to Him? If you haven't, what are you waiting for, friend? Trust in His everlasting love for you.

Only a supernatural
love transforms
hearts and renews
the minds
of so many.

Horace Holloways Jr.

REFINING FIRE QUESTIONS

Recall a moment when you experienced God's love. What did He do? Be prepared to pass along that same love to someone else when the time is right.

_____

_____

_____

What lessons have you learned in the "schoolroom of suffering?" What evidence do you see in your life from the lessons learned?

_____

_____

_____

Has your love for God become lukewarm? Does the fire to serve Him still burn hot? What are you doing to show Him your love?

_____

_____

_____

> For I am convinced that neither death, nor life, nor angels, nor principalities, nor things present, nor things to come, nor powers, nor height, nor depth, nor any other created thing, will be able to separate us from the love of God, which is in Christ Jesus our Lord.
>
> Romans 8:38–39

7

GOD USES OUR PAIN AND SUFFERING TO

DEEPEN OUR COMMITMENT TO HIM

My fiancée stopped by my office to drop off a greeting card with some beautifully handwritten words tucked inside to express how deeply she loved me. We sometimes took a basket of food that she had lovingly prepared and had a romantic picnic in the park. The sun set, and the stars began to illuminate the evening sky.

I once drove a few hours to visit her at college for Valentine's Day weekend. I had not seen her since Christmas break. She was elated when I arrived. She bounded out of her dormitory, jumping up and down with overflowing joy and a smile as big as the world. These are a few of the memories that I hold dearly in my heart as I remember my former fiancée. Her enthusiastic love for me made me love her even more.

When we recognize everything that God is doing in our lives and how He wants to transform our hearts and draw us closer to Him, our commitment to Him deepens. God has redeemed us.

God is using the pain in our lives to restore us. He is refining us to be used by Him. His reproofs may be painful, but they serve a divine purpose.

How can our love for Him not grow deeper every day?

I don't know what pain you're feeling now or have been carrying around with you over the years. I do know that you have a God who loves you, who is just and righteous, and who is holy with infinite wisdom. A God who, from the moment you were born, desires an intimate relationship with you.

Are you living with a heart of gratitude toward God in the midst of your difficult and painful circumstances?

Anne Graham Lotz is the daughter of the renowned preacher, evangelist, and Bible teacher Billy Graham. (May he rest in peace.) I am blessed by her words, especially after publishing my book on the power of prayer and reading excerpts from her prayer book in my devotions.

In one of her recent books, *The Daniel Prayer*, Anne reminds us how easy it would have been for Daniel to wonder where God was in his life. He became a slave in a faraway land, ripped from his family and all that was familiar to him. Even when God elevated Daniel in a foreign country, many wanted harm to come to him. However, Daniel still made it his priority to serve almighty God and talk with Him three times a day without fail.[8]

Anne writes, "Daniel's attitude illustrates one of the great secrets to trusting God. The key to thankfulness is not to view God through the lens of our circumstances, but to view our circumstances through the lens of God's love and sovereign purpose. God had not called Daniel to a life of comfort and ease, but to a life of greatness."[9]

Our love for God should deepen naturally as we endure trials and tests in our lives.

---

8 Anne Graham Lotz, *The Daniel Prayer: Prayer That Moves Heaven and Changes Nations*, (Grand Rapids: Zondervan, 2016).
9 Lotz, *The Daniel Prayer*, 39.

Developing Our Love for Him on a Daily Basis

These three things will further intensify our commitment to God and show Him how much we love Him.

PRAYER

Don't let this word scare you or make you fearful. I absolutely cherish prayer. Prayer is the privilege and the blessing of being able to communicate with God at any time. Prayer draws us closer to Him. The more we talk with God, the stronger our love for Him grows and the more we enjoy our time with Him. We are connecting with our Savior on a personal level.

We recognize His forgiveness of our sins; we appreciate the faith He has blessed us with to accept Him as our Lord and Savior. We thank Him for the undeserved grace and mercy bestowed on us. The Holy Spirit lives within our hearts, convicting, strengthening, and comforting us.

These are just a few of the things that God has revealed to me in my painful circumstances. Whatever we are doing—crying out to Him in our pain, seeking wisdom and direction when things are confusing. Or maybe even attempting to do His will—we can always talk with God about anything.

Romans 12:12 is one of my new favorite Bible verses regarding prayer, and it's so easy to remember, even for someone like me with a traumatic brain injury. "Rejoicing in hope, persevering in tribulation, devoted to prayer."

This is a short but powerful description of how to live as Christians from the apostle Paul. As we experience painful and difficult circumstances, we should live with the joy that only Christ can provide.

Even before my stroke, when I was living in sin and not seeking God consistently, I confessed my sins to Him most mornings. However, I did not repent for those sins. No change was taking place in my heart. God had to stop the perpetual cycle of rebellious sin and put me on the path of living for Him.

Now I approach His throne of grace with a repentant heart, and He is working to develop my faith from strong to exquisite. I aspire to daily experience a trust without doubt and fear lingering in my mind. Read these words of instruction from the Lord. "Call upon Me in the day of trouble; I shall rescue you, and you will honor Me" (Psalm 50:15).

As I lay in that hospital room with a river of tears cascading down my face after being physically abused in my first rehab facility, I called upon God, repeatedly pleading with Him to help me. I also asked Him to forgive me for living so selfishly and disobediently. It is my prayer going forward that I honor God by the life that I now live and the testimony of my faith in Him.

OBEDIENCE

Even more than the word "prayer," I believe this word makes some Christians uncomfortable. Now you may ask yourself, "Why is obedience so important?" Well, Adam and Eve in the garden of Eden can shed some light on the answer. Think about what their disobedience cost them. Think about what their disobedience cost even you and me to this day. Disobedience is sin, and sin separates us from God.

One way we can easily disobey God is by refusing to wait. I know, one of our favorite words, right? I have struggled with patience for as long as I can remember. It got to the point where I would, at times, be visibly upset if I were forced to wait for anything.

I believe God has had me in a season of waiting for several years (and counting). He is teaching me patience and reminding me to put my complete trust in Him. From the moment I was in the hospital after my stroke, I have especially been forced to wait.

For a go-getter like me, waiting has been tough. While in the hospital, I had to wait for help from the nurses. (They were amazing, by the way.) I had to wait patiently for my meals. Even during physical therapy, I had to wait for the therapists because they were helping more than one patient at a time.

After writing an award-winning book on prayer in 2016, I felt led by God to write more books and become a full-time author. I had some ideas for topics, but God wanted me to wait for His timing. I'll never forget the joy I felt when He gave me the title for this book during a quiet moment with Him.

The more emails and notes I began to receive from readers, the more I understood how God's timing played into my life. He showed me how much people were hurting, and my desire to point them to Jesus became even stronger.

Here are some of my favorite verses of Scripture regarding waiting on God. Please read these scriptures out loud, and focus on what God is saying to us.

"I would have despaired unless I believed that I would see the goodness of the Lord in the land of the living. Wait for the Lord; be strong and let your heart take courage; yes, wait for the Lord" (Psalm 27:13–14).

"For from days of old they have not heard or perceived by ear, nor has the eye seen a God besides You, *who acts on behalf of the one who waits for him*" (Isaiah 64:4, emphasis added).

"Rest in the Lord and wait patiently for Him; do not fret because of him who prospers in his way" (Psalms 37:7).

"The Lord is good to those who wait for Him. To the person who seeks Him" (Lamentations 3:25).

"Those who wait for the Lord will gain new strength; they will mount up with wings like eagles, they will run and not get tired, they will walk and not become weary" (Isaiah 40:31).

It takes courageous faith to wait on God, especially during painfully confusing and difficult circumstances. When we are seeking to do His will, we might not understand why God's schedule is not the same as ours. We wonder if He has forgotten about us and our situation. I assure you that this is not the case. God is concerned about every minute detail of our lives.

"O Lord, You have searched me and known me. You know when I sit down and when I rise up; You understand my thought from afar. You scrutinize my path and my lying down, and are intimately acquainted with all my ways" (Psalm 139:1–3).

One thing I have been waiting on since my stroke is a car. Mine was totaled while I was in rehab. I have been praying for almost nine years for God to bless me with a new one.

After searching for wisdom in His word, I understand that this is my time of waiting—just like it was for Moses in the desert, the apostle Paul before his missionary journeys, and Joseph who was forced to remain in prison for something he did not do.

I miss the independence of having my own vehicle. However, I appreciate the help and fellowship of those who have picked me up for church and driven me to the doctor or the grocery store.

My life may not have the same impact on others as the lives of those stalwarts from the Bible did, but God has specific purposes that are uniquely intended for me—testimonies of faith that only I can share.

As I spent more and more time waiting in the hospital, God began to chip away at the rough edges of my heart. I could not move around much, so I spent a lot of time staring at the tiles on the ceiling.

My mother had brought a radio for me. It was on a Christian station all the time—KCBI 90.9. I believe the station's tagline at the time was "a message of hope." Listening to the Bible teachings and worship music was so comforting. I began to single out some of my favorite preachers. I call them my spiritual "fantastic four."

- Dr. Tony Evans, pastor of Oak Cliff Bible Fellowship in Dallas, Texas
- Dr. Robert Jeffress, pastor of First Baptist Church in Dallas, Texas
- Dr. David Jeremiah, pastor of Shadow Mountain Community Church in San Diego, California
- Dr. Charles Stanley, pastor of First Baptist Church in Atlanta, Georgia

These men of God and their biblical teachings have helped me tremendously in my desire to live a Christ-like life since my stroke.

I began watching their messages on television too. I was still unable to walk, and I could barely sit up at the time, so I was thankful that they showed the Scriptures on the screen instead of just waving the Bible in the air. I was hungry to learn all I could about living for God, and I wanted to take advantage of this opportunity I'd been given to serve Him.

One of the pastors that first caught my attention was local. His teaching was easy for me to understand, and what he said made a lot of sense. My heart was inspired. I said to myself, "When I can walk again, I am going to attend First Baptist Dallas, sit in the front row, and recommit my life to Christ."

By the grace of God, that's precisely what happened on September 9, 2012. At the end of the service, I stood up and shook Pastor Jeffress's hand and said I wanted to rededicate my life to Christ.

After the church service was over, I met with the staff to confirm my recommitment. I had some pictures taken of me standing in the sanctuary after most people had left. The pure joy of recommitting my life to Christ and standing there in church just two years after my stroke was exhilarating.

In his 2018 book, *Choosing the Extraordinary Life*, Dr. Jeffress shares some insights on waiting on God that resonate strongly with me.

> "God is not in the habit of revealing his entire plan for our
> life all at once. If He did, we would race forward without

ever feeling the need to slow down, listen to his voice, and wait for His direction."[10]

That is why God's Word is a light unto our feet (Psalm 119:105, author's paraphrase). He gives just enough light for us to take the next step in faith. When we refuse to wait on Him, we are saying that we know better than God does and that we don't trust Him. Taking that path, my friend, will lead us directly into the furnace of affliction.

SERVICE

This is the final piece of the puzzle in deepening our commitment to Christ. We are communicating with God on a consistent basis, we have surrendered our hearts to obey Him in every circumstance, and now it is time for us to serve.

Four years ago, I decided to create a website to share my testimony of faith in hopes of encouraging those who visited. I prayed about the name of my site for weeks. Initially, I wanted something referencing salt and light, but God gave me another answer—pleasingtothepotter.com. I loved this title because it represented how I wanted to live my life going forward—pleasing Him. God continues to mold and transform me into the man He desires.

In the early stages of my site, a dedicated group of Christian women left comments on my blog posts, stating, "May God bless you in your ministry."

At the time, I thought, *ministry? I don't have a ministry; I just love to write.* However, over time, I began to realize that writing is my ministry. I can reach people for Christ all over the world with just a few taps on my keyboard.

God may not call us to preach to hundreds of people every week, but we can serve Him in our sphere of influence every day. If you're a homemaker or a parent, He is using you to shape the lives of your children. If you are a

---

10 Dr. Robert Jeffress, *Choosing the Extraordinary Life: God's 7 Secrets For Success And Significance* (Grand Rapids: Baker Publishing Group, 2018), 96.

teacher, a civil servant, or even a mail carrier, God can use you for His glory as His representative as well.

From the moment my father told me when I was eleven years old that God had called him to be a preacher, I rebelled until the time I left home. I wanted him to know that I wanted no part of being a missionary pastor's son.

Despite my repeated acts of defiance as a teenager, my father showed me loving-kindness and gentleness, which I will always remember. Yes, he disciplined me at times, but his spirit of compassion and his willingness to help me without question strengthens the love I have for him.

Now, my heart aches with sorrow as his body and mind slowly deteriorate in his horrific fight against Alzheimer's disease. I'm heartbroken that we can no longer have those discussions that he longed to have with me about the Bible, Christianity, and God.

Oh, how I wish he could read and understand my books as I seek to glorify God. I would give anything to call my dad on the phone, ask him biblical questions, and hear his feedback on something I've written.

But instead of looking at this situation and allowing discouragement to set in, I am focusing on being available to serve the Lord in whichever way He chooses, and right now, that is through my writing.

You can do the same in everything you do. Regardless of the role you play, God wants you to be willing to serve Him. He may even move circumstances around to point you in the direction He desires.

The circumstance may be unexpected and even painful, but it is all part of God's purpose for you. After returning to work following my stroke, I was terminated a year later. I was stunned and deeply hurt at the time. A few months afterward, God inspired me through my baby sister to do what I always wanted to do—write. In this moment, I cannot think of anything else I'd rather do than write and speak about my Savior.

Prayer. Obedience. Service. These are three powerful ways our commitment to God deepens, our love for Him grows stronger, and Christ becomes more evident in our lives.

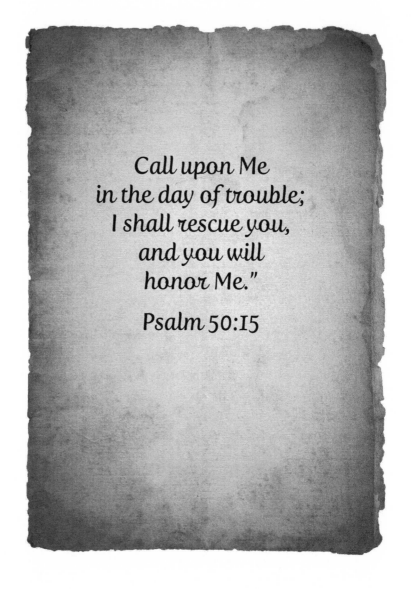

Call upon Me
in the day of trouble;
I shall rescue you,
and you will
honor Me."

Psalm 50:15

REFINING FIRE QUESTIONS

Are you living with a thankful heart in the midst of your painful or difficult circumstances? If not, how can you make that change?

_____

_____

_____

Which areas of your life need work in deepening your commitment to God? Prayer? Obedience? Service? What changes can you make right now?

_____

_____

_____

What areas of your life have you been unwilling to surrender to God? When will you be willing to make a change? Make those adjustments now.

_____

_____

_____

If your law had not been my delight, then I would have
perished in my affliction. I will never forget Your precepts,
for by them you have revived me. I am Yours, save me;
for I have sought your precepts.

Psalm 119:92–94

8

GOD USES OUR PAIN AND SUFFERING TO

DELIVER HOPE, COMFORT, AND JOY

One afternoon, after I had endured rigorous rounds of physical, occupational, and speech therapy at the hospital, a nurse peeked into my room and stated that an ambulance was on the way to pick me up at seven o'clock that evening. Since my insurance had run out, I was forced to move on. Move on to where?

Six weeks had passed since my stroke, and I had to celebrate my forty-fourth birthday in the hospital. Though God had blessed me with an uplifting surprise birthday party with family and friends, after the news from the nurse, I was not feeling much joy at all.

My mother was scrambling to locate a rehabilitation facility that could take in an overweight patient at the last minute. I had lost almost 150 pounds in the hospital, but I was still over the weight limit for many rehab facilities.

My family and I were anxious as to where the next phase of my recovery would begin. I was still unable to walk, and my eyesight had been adversely affected by the stroke. However, God provided me with a rehab facility near my parents' home.

With everything happening at that moment, I still had hope. (That being said, I was scared out of my mind.)

Even though I was aware that my move wasn't because of an improvement in my health, I knew that God was slowly but surely drawing me back to Him. Sometimes God has to break you to provide you with the blessings He wants to bestow. "Remember the word to Your servant, in which you have made me hope. *This is my comfort in my affliction, that Your Word has revived me*" (Psalm 119:49–50, emphasis added).

For years, I had put my confidence in my finances, talents, and abilities. Unfortunately, I had repeatedly ignored the fact that it was God who blessed me with each of those things.

My talents and abilities landed me flat on my back, struggling to move my body in even the simplest of ways. However, now my hope was in almighty God, the Creator of heaven and earth and Lord of my heart.

Joy is more than happiness based on an outcome or circumstance. Joy is the supernatural delight in God's purpose for our lives. Joy is something that God offers us in the midst of our pain and suffering. We must choose to live with joy. "But as for me, I shall sing of Your strength; Yes, I shall joyfully sing of Your lovingkindness every morning, for You have been my stronghold and a refuge in the day of my distress" (Psalm 59:16).

When we embrace God-infused joy, we experience peace. At the end of every sermon at my new church, Matthew Road Baptist Church, Pastor Daniel bids us Godspeed with a quotation from Scripture. It is a passage of hope and comfort. This Scripture was the benediction that God instructed Moses to give to Aaron to bless His people. "The Lord bless you, and keep you; the Lord make His face shine on you and be gracious to you; the Lord lift up His countenance on you, and give you peace" (Numbers 6:24–26).

Can you imagine the ultimate warmth of God's face shining on you? No other peace can match that from our Father in heaven. (Philippians 4:7, author's paraphrase)

After rededicating my life to Christ, I committed to reading through the Bible in its entirety because I did not want to miss anything God had to say to me. I've learned that the Old Testament has numerous treasures, and we can discover so much as we seek to live for Him.

I have continued to read the Bible. I am now in my sixth straight year of reading through it from cover to cover (including Leviticus, but I digress). Whatever painful trial or difficulty we may be experiencing, God wants to give us indescribable hope and incomparable peace.

God uses pain and suffering to prepare us. Not only is He preparing us for our eternity in heaven with Him but He is designing us to be used for His glory right here and now in our everyday lives. "You are the light of the world. A city set on a hill cannot be hidden; nor does anyone light a lamp and put it under a basket, but on the lampstand, and it gives light to all who are in the house" (Matthew 5:14–15).

Earlier in this book, I shared 2 Corinthians 1:4, which states that God comforts us in our afflictions so that we can comfort others. It's my prayer that He uses my testimony to comfort and encourage you, giving you hope that no matter the painful circumstances or trying times you experience, God will bring you through.

STEADFAST HOPE

The apostle Paul is the greatest missionary in history. He wrote almost half of the New Testament. It is remarkable how God transformed his life from who he was as Saul.

That is why I am so amazed at just how many Scriptures of exhortation, instruction, and encouragement that are infused by the Holy Spirit come to us through Paul. God can take our weaknesses and make them strengths (2 Corinthians 12:10, author's paraphrase).

He can turn our pain into a platform for His glory, be that pain physical, emotional, or spiritual. We can be a light shining brightly where God has us, affecting lives and changing hearts through God's transforming power. Read this encouraging passage that Paul wrote to the Christians at the church in Thessalonica.

We give thanks to God always for all of you, making mention of you in our prayers; constantly bearing in mind, your work of faith and labor of love and *steadfastness of hope in our Lord Jesus Christ* in the presence of our God and Father, knowing, brethren beloved by God, His choice of you; for our gospel did not come to you in word only, but also in power and in the Holy Spirit with full conviction; just as you know what kind of men we proved to be among you for your sake. *You also became imitators of us and of the Lord, having received the word in much tribulation with the joy of the Holy Spirit, so that you became an example to all the believers in Macedonia and Achaia* (1 Thessalonians 1:2–7, emphasis added).

Chances are good that you and I will never meet. If you know Christ as your Lord and Savior, though, we will worship together in heaven someday. I want you to know that I will be praying for those who read this book—praying that you know that God has a divine plan and purpose for everything and that you find comfort in your times of need and hope during your painful moments of distress.

God's purpose is for us as Christians to live as imitators of Jesus Christ. He wants us to be living, breathing examples of what it means to live for Him. His plan for us is not to always live comfortably but to live intentionally for Him.

GLORIFYING GOD

We have the opportunity and the privilege to bring glory to God in the midst of our pain and suffering. It may not feel like that is the case during the time of our hurts, but as heirs of Christ, we can always glorify the Lord.

"The Spirit Himself testifies with our spirit that we are children of God, and if children, heirs also, heirs of God and fellow heirs with Christ. If indeed we suffer with Him so that we may also be glorified with Him. For I consider that the sufferings of this present time are not worthy to be compared with the glory that is to be revealed to us" (Romans 8:16–18).

If you are familiar with the New Testament, then you've heard of the apostle Peter. He was one of the first men who Jesus requested to follow Him and become a disciple. Peter loved the Lord deeply.

His passionate temperament got him in trouble at times. He had the chance to walk out on the water and meet Jesus, but he looked down at the stormy waves underneath his feet, taking his eyes off Jesus, and began to sink. Jesus reached out, pulled him up, and questioned his faith (Matthew 14:28–31, author's paraphrase).

In the garden of Gethsemane, where Judas Iscariot betrayed Jesus before His crucifixion, Peter used a sword to cut off a guard's ear, which Jesus reattached. (See John 18:10–11).

One of the more infamous events in Peter's life occurred just a few hours after the incident in Gethsemane. While Jesus was being accused, interrogated, and mistreated after His arrest, Peter was in the courtyard denying that he knew Jesus. "But Peter said, "Man I do not know what you are talking about." Immediately, while he was still speaking, a rooster crowed. The Lord turned and looked at Peter. And Peter remembered the word of the Lord, how He had told him, "Before a rooster crows today, you will deny Me three times." And he went out and wept bitterly" (Luke 22: 60–62).

I cannot begin to imagine how devastating Peter's pain must have been when he and Jesus' eyes met on that fateful night. Peter had been by His side, serving in ministry for three years. However, at that moment of truth, he was not bringing glory to God at all.

The beauty of serving a God who loves us unconditionally is that this wasn't the end of Peter's story. Peter was invited with James and John to witness the transfiguration of Christ, which took place on the Mount of Olives. After Christ rose from the grave, He saw Peter on multiple occasions.

Peter was also one of the founding apostles of the first Christian church. His initial sermon, infused by the Holy Spirit, resulted in the salvation of over three thousand souls (Acts 2:41).

He was someone just like you and me who God desired to use for His purpose—someone who loved the Lord but in the humanness of his flesh fell short at times.

In the spring of 2017, I was in pain while sitting in church when I heard the following challenging words from the apostle Peter. I began to weep so profusely that my nephew had to run out and grab a box of tissues for me.

> *Beloved, do not be surprised at the fiery ordeal among you, which comes upon you for your testing, as though some strange thing were happening to you; but to the degree that you share the sufferings of Christ, keep on rejoicing, so that also at the revelation of His glory you may rejoice with exultation.* If you are reviled for the name of Christ, you are blessed, because the Spirit of glory and of God rests on you. Make sure that none of you suffers as a murderer, or thief, or evildoer, or as a troublesome meddler, but if anyone suffers as a Christian, he is not to be ashamed, but is to glorify God in this name . . . . *Therefore, those also who suffer according to the will of God shall entrust their souls to a faithful Creator in doing what is right* (1 Peter 4:12–16, 19, emphasis added).

As chosen members of God's family, we have the opportunity to glorify Him in our pain and suffering. We can give hope to those who come in contact with us and who watch us from a distance. Every day of our lives, we glorify God by how we behave—especially when we are hurting. Look at these Old Testament words of praise from the prophet Habakkuk.

"Though the fig tree should not blossom and there be no fruit on the vines, though the yield of the olive should fail and the fields produce no food, though the flock should be cut off from the fold and there be no cattle in the stalls, yet I will exult in the Lord, I will rejoice in the God of my salvation. The Lord God is my strength, and He has made my feet like hinds' feet, and makes me walk on my high places" (Habakkuk 3:17–19).

Our rejoicing in our painful trials brings glory to God. Jesus Christ is the epicenter of our confession of faith, but salvation should also affect how we live each day. We are comforted, knowing that each trial in our lives has a divine purpose.

We are not alone in times of pain and suffering. God is with us every excruciating step of the way. He is preparing us for glory, and knowing this, we can have hope.

My body was broken after my stroke. I was unsure if I would ever walk again, but I was consumed with a voracious hunger to draw nearer to my Savior. I wanted to talk with Him and hear from Him.

I would fall asleep at times, praying, asking Him for the strength to endure my rehab for another day. My injured mind and body were drained, but I had hope. At times during my recovery, I felt envious of those in therapy who were further along than I was. One important thing I've learned is that God's timing is perfect.

After an extremely trying time at one rehabilitation facility, God blessed me with Christian physical therapists who pushed me outside my comfort zone. One therapist in particular, Rachel Atkins, drove me beyond what I thought was possible, but she celebrated my progression with joy.

I wheeled myself into the gym; it was finally time to attempt walking between the parallel bars. At that time, I felt as if I were gazing at Mount Everest. I rose to my feet on my shaky legs. My crumpled left hand gripped one bar, and my right hand gripped the other. My injured left leg felt as if it weighed a ton when I picked it up.

Then it happened—a baby step on the right foot slowly followed by one on the left foot while Rachel supported me with a gait belt around my waist. She was with me all the way. Day after day, week after week, and month after month, she was there to guide, instruct, and encourage me to press forward. Despite the pain and fear I experienced, she refused to let me give up.

At times, I had no idea why she was asking me to do certain things during rehab. Sometimes I felt so alone when she instructed me to roll my wheelchair or walk my walker down the long and winding corridors on my own.

What I did not know was that she had assigned people to keep an eye on me throughout this process, and I was never really alone. My body grew stronger over time, my spirit improved, and I eventually retrained myself to walk. I begin to listen to her daily instructions with eagerness.

We may never understand all that God is taking us through, but we are not supposed to grasp every little thing. If we knew it all, why would we need God?

We have to guard against making the same mistake Adam and Eve did in the garden. We do not need to know everything when the God of the universe has chosen us and welcomed us into His family.

He is preparing us to be his vessel. Do we want to be that vessel He is forced to leave on the shelf because we are not living the way He has intended us to live, or do we desire to be a beautiful, radiant vessel that God can use to glorify Him?

> For God, who said, "Light shall shine out of darkness," is the One who has shone in our hearts to give the Light of the knowledge of the glory of God in the face of Christ. But we have this treasure in earthen vessels, so that the surpassing greatness of the power will be the will of God and not from ourselves; *we are afflicted in every way, but not crushed; perplexed, but not despairing; persecuted, but not forsaken; struck down, but not destroyed; always carrying about in the body the dying of Jesus, so that the life of Jesus also may be manifested in our body* . . . . Therefore we do not lose heart, but though our outer man is decaying, yet our inner man is being renewed day by day. *For momentary, light affliction is producing for us an eternal weight of glory far beyond all comparison*, while we look not at the things which are seen, but at the things which are not seen; for the things which are seen are temporal, but the things which are not seen are eternal (2 Corinthians 4: 6–10, 16–18).

Just as God had a purpose with Adam and Eve, He has a purpose for all Christians—to live with Him in perfect harmony someday. Every painful trial, tribulation, and thorn is part of the process of preparing us for eternal glory with Jesus Christ, our Savior.

The glory that we will receive in heaven is beyond anything that we can ever imagine. Streets covered in brilliant gold. A home prepared by Jesus uniquely designed for us (John 14:2). Crowns awarded to us for our service to Him. The praise and worship of multitudes glorifying God will be incredible!

Looking toward our future is how we can have hope and live with joy and peace amid our suffering.

God is preparing us for eternal glory with Him. Our upcoming time in heaven should be our focus during our painful circumstances. Read this promise from God regarding pain in heaven. "And He will wipe away every tear from their eyes; and there will no longer be any death; there will no longer be any mourning, or crying, or pain; the first things have passed away" (Revelation 21:4).

A huge smile takes over my face when I think about spending eternity with my Lord and Savior. I have every confidence that God is shaping me to fit His plan and purpose for the time He has blessed me with here on earth.

Experiencing joy doesn't mean that I no longer experience pain. Instead, it means that God is bringing me to a place where I now have the inclination to ask Him, "What do You want me to see in this distressing circumstance, Lord?"

MOVING FORWARD

The apostle Paul experienced being beaten within inches of his life; stoned and left for dead; shipwrecked; and imprisoned on multiple occasions. One of the things that I appreciate about his writing is his boldness in serving Christ. He has given us a perfect way to look at life as we move forward. In reading these verses of Scripture, permit them to encourage and challenge your heart.

But whatever things were gain to me, those things I have

counted as loss for the sake of Christ. More than that, I count all things to be a loss in view of the surpassing value of knowing Christ Jesus my Lord, for whom I have suffered the loss of all things, and count them but rubbish so that I may gain Christ, and be found in Him . . . *that I may know Him and the power of His resurrection and the fellowship of His sufferings* . . . Not that I have already obtained it or have already become perfect, but I press on so that I may lay hold of that for which also I was laid hold of by Christ Jesus. Brethren, I do not regard myself as having laid hold of it yet; but one thing I do: *Forgetting what lies behind and reaching forward to what lies ahead, I press on toward to the goal for the prize of the upward call of God in Christ Jesus* (Philippians 3:7–8, 10, 12–14, emphasis added).

Here is my challenge for us going forward.

Let's live in a way that glorifies God and does not force Him to use pain to get our attention. Let's refuse to allow our painful circumstances to define us; instead, let's allow them to develop us.

We need to listen for the whispers of our Savior who loves us and be prepared to willingly live out His desires until He calls us home. Are you ready and willing to fulfill God's purposes for your life? "To this end, also we pray for you always, that our God will count you worthy of your calling, and fulfill every desire for goodness and the work of faith with power, so that the name of our Lord Jesus will be glorified in you, and you in Him, according to the grace of our God and the Lord Jesus Christ" (2 Thessalonians 1:11–12).

"Now may our Lord Jesus Christ Himself and God our Father, who has loved us and given us eternal comfort and good hope by grace, comfort and strengthen your hearts in every good work and word" (2 Thessalonians 2:16–17).

"Blessed is a man who perseveres under trial; for once he has been approved, he will receive the crown of life which the Lord has promised to those who love Him" (James 1:12).

A FINAL STORY

Knowing God is more than book knowledge—it is experiencing God to the fullest. James writes that even the demons believe in God (James 2:19, author's paraphrase).

Nine years had passed since the breakup with my fiancée, and I started spending quality time with another beautiful Christian woman.

This woman challenged me to think outside the box. She opened my eyes to things outside sports events, food, and movies. We once went to the lake for the day. She showed me how to start a campfire and bake a potato in the ground. (It was delicious!)

Another time, she wanted to take me to the symphony. I'm sure my face looked like I'd sucked on a lemon because she immediately burst into laughter. She plays an instrument, but I had given up playing the piano when I was a teenager, so I was not looking forward to an evening at the symphony. In fact, even though my father has always loved classical music, I did not understand it at all. I thought it was music to help you fall asleep.

In my effort to please her, I agreed to go with her. She was overjoyed and said she would take care of everything. The evening of the performance, I picked her up, and we headed to the symphony, but when we arrived, I felt out of place right away.

Everyone was elegantly dressed. It was like a bunch of grown-ups going to the prom—shiny shoes, tuxedos, dresses that glittered. We entered the softly lit performance hall, and the musicians were tuning their instruments and warming up. It seemed as if we were on hallowed ground as we whispered to each other high up in the balcony.

I felt less uncomfortable as I saw the gleam in her eyes. She was thrilled to be there, which made me happy. I looked down at my program and did not recognize much of the music they'd be playing.

The lights in the balcony dimmed, the conductor made his way to the front of the orchestra, and a gentle round of applause echoed throughout the concert hall.

As the conductor raised his hands and the musicians began to play, something familiar met my eardrums. I listened more intently, leaning forward and then looking at my program again.

I recognized the music! The pieces were from musical scores of movies I'd watched and enjoyed. Now I was just as thrilled to be there as my companion was. My eyes were gleaming like hers, and I whispered to her that I knew the songs. She saw my genuine excitement and smiled sweetly as she held my hand. I listened closely to every song, trying to place each one, eager to see if I'd recognize more. It was one of the best experiences I've ever had on a date!

Maybe my father wasn't crazy after all. Classical music is beautiful. That evening, I experienced the effects of the exquisite sounds instead of just having knowledge of them. All the various instruments coming together in harmony were spectacular! Nowadays, especially when I'm writing articles about my father, I enjoy playing classical music. It helps me connect and remember my moments with him, and I become overwhelmed by emotions at times.

Experiencing Christ involves suffering. Jesus was ridiculed, beaten, spat upon, and brutally hung on a cross at the demand of those He had healed and comforted during His ministry. He rose from the grave three days later and now sits in glory at the right hand of God, anticipating the day when we will join Him in heaven. His sacrifice gives us the opportunity to live for Him as His children.

In the depths of our pain and suffering, we must continue pressing forward to do the will of God for our lives. We need to live for Christ with steadfast courage despite the painful and trying circumstances we face.

God's purposes give us incomprehensible hope. We should live our lives with joyful confidence, knowing that ongoing suffering and every painful experience are a part of His perfect plan. Let the pain move us toward an excellent faith, understanding that we have been chosen by God to serve Him.

Joy is the supernatural delight in God's purpose for our lives. Joy is something that God offers us in the midst of our pain and suffering. We must choose to live with joy.

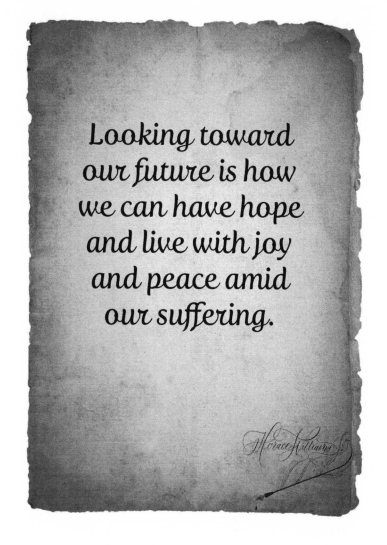

Looking toward our future is how we can have hope and live with joy and peace amid our suffering.

REFINING FIRE QUESTIONS

Are you living with joyful hope in Christ? If so, list the ways you are. If not, what changes do you need to make to begin doing so?

_____

_____

_____

When faced with painful and difficult times, do you live as a victim of your circumstances or as a victor in Christ Jesus? How is this fulfilling God's purpose for you?

_____

_____

_____

What do people see in you? How can you show that you are a joyous Christian who lives in eager expectation of glory?

_____

_____

_____

The steadfast of mind You will keep in perfect peace, because he trusts in You. Trust in the Lord forever, for in God the Lord we have an everlasting Rock.

Isaiah 26:3–4

Looking for the blessed hope and the appearing of the glory of our great God and Savior, Christ Jesus who gave Himself for us to redeem us from every lawless deed, and to purify for Himself a people for his own possession, zealous for good deeds.

Titus 2:13–14

CONCLUSION

Friend, I am not sure where you are in the furnace of affliction and what God is trying to accomplish in your life. He may want to purify you from some habitual or sneaky sins. Or maybe He is restoring your faith in Him as you experience painful and difficult trials and testing. I do know that He is refining you and preparing you for service and the glory that awaits.

Writing this book has been challenging for me at times as I remember some of the most painful moments in my life, but I have a sincere desire to help those of you who are hurting. I believe this is God's purpose for me at this moment in time, to offer hope and encouragement for those who read what God puts on my heart.

You might never have suffered a stroke or battled a chronic physical illness, but I am sure that at some point in your life, you have experienced pain. As children of God, all of us will experience some form of pain here on earth.

PURIFICATION. RESTORATION. REFINING. PREPARATION.

These things take place in the life of every Christian. Each stage is an essential part through the process of sanctification. God is preparing us not only to live as salt and light while we are here on earth but also to stand before the King of Kings as we worship Him in heaven someday! This is God's ultimate purpose. "Now may the God of Peace Himself sanctify you entirely; and may your spirit and soul and body be preserved complete, without blame at the coming of our Lord Jesus Christ. Faithful is He who calls you, and He will also bring it to pass" (1 Thessalonians 5:23–24).

Pain and suffering are necessary during the process of sanctifying God's saints. Let's not be dull of hearing as we live the Christian life (Hebrews 5:11, author's paraphrase), forcing God to put us in the furnace which delays how and when He can use us.

For me, forty-one years had passed from the time I accepted Jesus as my Savior to the time I recommitted my life to Christ.

Being deaf to God's purposes doesn't affect only us. In my situation, my condition has profoundly and unexpectedly touched the lives of those I love; those closest to me have paid an extreme emotional toll as a result of my stroke.

However, in the midst of my pain and suffering, God remains faithful. He reveals His love for me in numerous ways and on countless occasions. God is always by my side, and God desires for you to experience His presence as He prepares you for service and glory. He has given us these Scriptures of hope from His Word.

> In the same way God, desiring even more to show to the heirs of the promise the unchangeableness of His purpose, interposed with an oath, that by two unchangeable things in which it is impossible for God to lie, we who have taken refuge would have strong encouragement to take hold of the hope set before us. *This hope we have as an anchor of the soul, a hope both sure and steadfast and one which enters within the veil, where Jesus has entered as a forerunner for us,* having become a high priest forever according to the order of Melchizedek (Hebrews 6:17–20, emphasis added).

Every promise and Scripture verse in this book is from a God who cannot lie. It is not in His nature to do so.

We have been chosen by an omnipotent, omniscient, omnipresent, and holy God to be an essential part of His family. For us to accomplish His will as a member of this most royal of families, God expects us, His children, to carry ourselves in a particular manner.

If we believe our ways are better, He will take corrective and sometimes extremely painful steps in preparing us to stand in the heavenly temple before the King of Kings. God uses these trials in the furnace of affliction because of His great love for us. "Blessed is the man who trusts in the Lord, and whose trust is in the Lord. For he will be like a tree planted by the water, that extends its roots by a stream and will not fear when the heat comes; but its leaves will be green, and it will not be anxious in a year of drought nor cease to yield fruit" (Jeremiah 17:7–8).

What a beautiful promise from our Father. Are we committing to putting our trust in Him in the midst of the searing trials and tribulations that affect our lives? Do our lives bear fruit that is pleasing to God and draws people to Christ?

JOY EVERLASTING!

Yes, I speak from experience. The trials and tests in life can be unexpected, devastating, tragic, and sometimes unexplainable, but that will be nothing in comparison to the joy that awaits us in heaven.

"Therefore we do not lose heart, but though our outer man is decaying, yet our inner man is being renewed day by day. For momentary, light affliction is producing for us an eternal weight of glory far beyond all comparison" (2 Corinthians 4:16–17).

I cannot encourage you enough to live life with joy, regardless of your circumstances—a joy based on the promises of a God who loves you unconditionally and wants what is best for you.

I know doing so is not easy, but God's purposes for us are intended for our good. His will for our lives will be accomplished, so we should make it easier on ourselves by drawing closer to Him. Seek His will daily, living a life that glorifies Him in everything we think, say, and do.

"For as the heavens are higher than the earth, so are My ways are higher than your ways and My thoughts than your thoughts. For as the rain and the snow come down from heaven, and do not return there without watering the earth and making it bear and sprout, and furnishing seed to the sower and bread to the eater; so will My word be which goes forth from My mouth; it will not return to Me empty, without accomplishing what I desire, and without succeeding in the matter for which I sent it" (Isaiah 55:9–11).

My parents scripted portions of these verses in the Bible they gave me almost a year before my stroke. I looked at the Bible, but promptly moved it out of sight (and as they say, out of mind).

Now, almost ten years later, the sword of the Spirit—that same Bible from my parents—is usually next to me, near the bed or on my desk, so that I can study. (I have a few versions of study Bibles in my home and a couple of Bible dictionaries as well.) This Bible now has highlighted Scriptures and several color-coded sticky notes throughout (and not a speck of dust to be seen). God continues to bless me with conviction, correction, encouragement, instruction, comfort, and joy from the pages of the Bible.

None of us are exempt from pain and suffering until we join our Savior, Jesus Christ, in heaven. However, knowing God's purposes should affect how we live our lives every day.

Every painful circumstance we experience is never a surprise to God. He is never caught napping or asleep at the wheel. God is our shepherd, and no matter where we are and what we are experiencing, He is *always* near. Everything must pass through the skillful hands of the Creator who made us, the Creator who knows everything about us and yet still loves us unconditionally.

We may even think that God has forgotten about us at times, and we feel forced to deal with our pain on our own. My friend, nothing could be further from the truth. We must remember to live and walk in faith and to not trust in only our feelings.

"For I am confident of this very thing, that He who began a good work in you will perfect it until the day of Christ Jesus" (Philippians 1:6).

God continues to work on us, using the furnace of affliction when necessary so He can use our lives and work through us for His glory.

"Things which eye has not seen and ear has not heard, and which have not entered the heart of man, all that God prepared for those who love Him" (1 Corinthians 2:9).

We must resolve in our hearts to be an integral part of God's purposes and not be dragged kicking and screaming to do His will. As children of God, we have been called into ministry, regardless of our occupation. "But you, be sober in all things, endure hardship, do the work of an evangelist, fulfill your ministry" (2 Timothy 4:5).

So let's rely on God's strength to serve our Savior with joy and be the shining examples of what the Christian faith looks like in both good times and bad. May we be a beacon of hope—a beacon that draws people to Christ Jesus—and live with the expectation of the indescribable glory that awaits us.

Are you ready to join me in living out God's purpose for our lives? We must not allow our time in the furnace to be for naught. Let's glorify Christ with our lives!

EPILOGUE

It was February of 2018 when I had my first conference call to discuss writing a book titled, *The Furnace of Affliction*. Over the months that followed, there were various attempts to thwart this book from being published. The enemy is REAL. On more than one occasion, I struggled mightily with doubt—BUT GOD. He would not let me give up or quit. The closer I got toward completing the book, I began to understand why it was necessary for me to write on this subject, at this time. I still battle daily with physical pain. Some days are worse than others. However, God continues to strengthen my faith and allow me to flourish in Him. My hope grows stronger every day as I seek to draw people to Christ. I want to share with you the hope of Jesus that lives within me. I know that 2020 has been a difficult and unprecedented year for most everyone. But it is my prayer that in reading this book you are reminded that God has a purpose in everything. So, keep your eyes on Him, and seek Him daily. Be well, friend, and God bless. You are never alone nor forgotten.

Resource Library

If you enjoyed the quotes at the end of each chapter, there are beautiful colored parchments with those same quotes in my Resource Library available for *FREE* download. Also, seven stunning printables titled Psalms of Hope, are there as well. A copy of the wedding vow I never got to say thirty years ago, and the poem I wrote after our engagement ended are also in the library.

https://www.pleasingtothepotter.com/resource-library/

Password: HOPE

Reviews are Appreciated!

If you love this book or even just liked it a little, now is the time when I would ask you to please go and leave a review wherever you bought it, or if you got a free copy, please do the same. Reviews are the lifeblood of books like this. And I would consider it a personal favor. I'm on a quest to get at least 500 reviews of this book, and I can only do it with your help.

You may also like my first book,
Unleash the Power of Prayer in Your Life.
Available at most major online retailers
where books are sold.

Made in the USA
Middletown, DE
20 June 2021